Right to the Money

The 7 Ways Wealthy Investors

Expand Their Success

Tony Hartman

Right to the Money

The 7 Ways Wealthy Investors Expand Their Success

ISBN: 9780615948072

Library of Congress Control Number: 2014902605

Right to the Money is a commonsense guide to personal finance and prosperity. In Right to the Money, as in life, there are no guarantees, and readers are cautioned to rely on their own judgment about their individual circumstances and to act accordingly. Nothing here should be interpreted as tax advice, legal advice, financial advice, investment advice, or medical advice.

Visit our website at www.RightToTheMoney.com

Printed in the United States of America

1st edition April 2014

Contents

Acknowledgements

There are always more people to thank who helped shape a new book (or shaped the author who writes the book) than can be named. So, let me start with a blanket thank you to everyone who contributed.

Special thanks go to my wife, Marina Hartman, without whose unending support, feedback and understanding this book would never have been written. Her suggestions and corrections were key to keeping me on path.

This book is also dedicated to my amazing children: Michelle, Mark, and Nicholas. You have given me purpose to look beyond today. Many days I think I learn more from you than what you learn from me. May this small book make a big difference in your life. You guys are my greatest inspiration.

And, to my parents, you taught me that I can overcome any of life's obstacles and that I can achieve anything I believe. Often your advice was very simple – work hard, think for yourself, don't spend money you don't have, do right by others, be self-reliant, grow at least some of your own food – but I believe those lessons provided the foundation for everything that has followed in my life. Your lessons shaped my life.

To Sean McCarthy, whose ideas contributed so much to my development as a person, an investor, and a private lender.

What Others Are Saying About This Book

"I have worked with Tony for a while now. He is unlike most investors. Tony has a true desire to help people live a better life. His approach to relationships is refreshing and cutting edge. Tony is one educator who can help you with a lot more than just your financial freedom in retirement; he can help you live a better life."

~Matthew Halloran, MS, Certified Life Coach

"You don't become wealthy unless you know how to handle your money. This book will guide you on your way."

~David Lindahl
Author "Emerging Real Estate Markets"

"Very informative and educational for the experienced investor and also for those who are just beginning to grow their wealth. Mr. Hartman has learned, and is able to explain, the strategies and keys to financial freedom and wealth within this short publication."

~John McGuire, Tax Attorney
McGuire Law Offices
McGuire Todd & Associates

"Tony's strategies are unconventional, especially when compared to most asset managers today; … his overall strategy is consistent with the wealth secrets outlined in his book."

~David Steckelberg
CPA, Brewer Tax and Accounting, Inc.

Introduction

Never at any time in all the history of mankind has there been more opportunities to build wealth and strategies to protect wealth. You can become a multi-millionaire or become as wealthy as you desire if you know how. Knowledge is one of the keys. But knowledge alone is not enough, just as wood is not enough to have a fire. It is better to view wealth as a way of thinking, an attitude or philosophy on how you approach life, and all of its promises, its problems, and its opportunities, mixed in with all of life's twists, turns, and surprises. Some call this part *Inner Game*. Summon your best Inner Game and expect to develop it, hone it, polish it, and use it as you improve your life.

There is an old Chinese proverb that says: "If you seek the way up the mountain, ask those who have gone there before." *Right to the Money* shows you little known and sometimes invisible strategies and techniques that others have taken to achieve their goals, to go up the money mountain. Have you ever seen a treasure map, all ragged and torn? What is such a treasure map worth? With action and proper Inner Game, its value can be equal to the value of the treasure located at the end of the map. *Right to the Money* is just like a treasure map, a map up the money mountain. The trail up the money mountain has been taken by others before you. The easiest way to achieve your goals and get up the money mountain is by taking the path that others have taken before. I say path because relative to the number of people in the world, not many have made much progress up the mountain. There is not an interstate highway or even a paved road up the mountain. No easy escalator button. But it is a clear path others have taken before you.

The path outlined here is easy. The hard part for most people is taking action. And, as people come in all different variations of skill and motivation, I imagine that some of these techniques will seem hard to do by some people. Even on this path – the easiest way up the mountain -- some people will think that parts of the trail are not just hard, but even insurmountable. If that applies to you, do not despair.

When you encounter adversity, it often just means you are making your way up the mountain and all you have to do is be persistent. It is part of our natural evolution to becoming better human beings. J. Paul Getty, a self-made *billionaire*, when speaking of adversity, once said: *"You should not only learn to handle adversity but to seek it out"*. Adversity can be a sign that you are making progress on your path to become a better, more highly evolved human being. This is one of the time-tested principles of progress. In fact, in the Chinese language the same symbol can be used to describe both "problem" and "opportunity". Napoleon Hill, in his best-selling novel throughout the decades – Think and Grow Rich – says that in every problem there lies the seed to an equal and greater opportunity. While at first glance you might disagree, with more thought you will realize that problems and opportunities are really the same thing. Problems and opportunities are two sides of the same coin. It is how people perceive and respond to a situation that determines which side of the coin they are focused on. Why do some people seem to be able to turn their problems into opportunities? Why is it that some people always manage to come out of problem situations "smelling like a rose"? The answer lies in persisting through the adversity, persisting through the problem, but focusing *on the opportunity*.

You can achieve financial independence by yourself, but that is not the easy way. Even the best known self-made millionaires – not only needed help – but actually sought out people to help them achieve their goals. This point is very important. It should even become a part of your Inner Game thinking. "How can I get others to help me"? Whether it is money, information, talent, or some resource – if you don't have it, somebody else does. You can develop your own source of resources. Or you can borrow resources from someone who already has it. This concept is using "people" leverage to help get what you want. This does not mean you exploit people. It means putting together win-win teams to accomplish a goal, organizing a mastermind group, hiring the experts (CPAs and attorneys) when you need them, hiring people to work with you, putting a good banker on your team, and helping others. Be the first person to deliver value in a relationship.

The amazing thing about *Right to the Money* is that for those who apply this knowledge, polish their Inner Game, and take action, they find themselves swept on to success – to the top of the money mountain – in an incredibly short period of time. You can use this powerful information to build and protect your wealth. You can also use it to put your life on the track that you want it on. You can make all of this happen regardless of where you are now. It's not where you are now that matters; it's where you are going that is important.

Many people – way too many people – struggle and settle for less than what they could be. For the life of me I do not know why. Perhaps it is because they don't know how. For you, lack of knowledge is no longer an excuse. Henry Ford once said that there are two kinds of knowledge in this world: general knowledge and specialized knowledge. General knowledge, no matter how much of it you have, will not help much in building and protecting wealth. Universities across the world are overflowing with general knowledge, yet do you know many mega-millionaire college professors? On the other hand, specialized knowledge is results oriented and much rarer than general knowledge. The proper use of specialized knowledge can literally build wealth and dramatically improve most any area of your life. *Right to the Money* is jam-packed with such specialized knowledge. Your next steps up the money mountain begin in this book.

Right to the Money

The 7 Ways Wealthy Investors

Expand Their Success

Chapter 1

Choose the Red Pill

One of my favorite movies is the popular film *'The Matrix'*. In a defining scene, Morpheus tells Neo about two choices he can make. Both will alter the course of his life:

1. Take the *Blue Pill* and the world remains the same as it is presented.
2. Take the *Red Pill* and learn how the world really works.

More than twenty years ago, I made a decision like this. I decided to take the *Red Pill* and to learn how the financial world really works. There are a great number of conventional financial strategies, but some of them that are espoused as gospel do not provide an accurate picture of the world as it really is. *Very Blue Pill.* When I took the *Red Pill* and got a better understanding of how the financial world really works, it changed the strategies I chose to use. Now I use strategies that were once only open to select hedge fund managers and private equity firms.

But here's the problem. It bothers me that there are so many people who have the *same viewpoint that once plagued me!* They don't understand the real world and how money works. Their *'Blue Pill'* mentality is like blinders that prevent them from seeing the full picture. It prevents them from getting all the success they deserve. It prevents them from having a *Right to the Money.*

The Truth is Simple

The world has changed dramatically, and some of the key assumptions you based your strategy choices on 20 or 30 years ago are no longer relevant. Worse, you didn't make any conscious financial decisions and just followed the herd. Continue on that path and you're severely limiting your chances of great success.

So I ask you to do a simple thing. Promise yourself that you're going to see the world for the way it really is. In other words, I want you to take the Red Pill and discover what's really going on.

Choosing the Red Pill can give you a *Slight Edge*. A *Slight Edge* is a small increment of improvement that can have an enormous impact on the end result. For example, in baseball a hitter who gets on base three out of 10 times, has a batting average of .300, and is considered good with the average ball player having an average of .255 in 2012[1]. But if a player gets on base one more time—four out of ten—his batting average is .400 and this player can earn millions of dollars more. He has a slight edge in batting that gets him on base one more time out of every ten at bats, yet it can mean many millions of dollars more in salary and endorsements.

The same can be said for professional golfers. There are thousands of outstanding amateurs who manage to break par from time to time. But they'll never make it to the professional level because there is an elite core of golfers who are simply more skilled and more consistent—not on every hole—not even on every round. But over time, they score, on average, just a few strokes per round better than the amateurs, but those few strokes make the difference between the professionals who may make millions of dollars over their career and the good amateurs who will never make the leap beyond their amateur status.

Even among the pros, the difference of a few strokes over a four-day, 72-hole tournament can make the difference between earning millions of dollars in winnings and earning just enough to cover their costs. Those who can beat the pack consistently—even by just a stroke or two—become the superstars of the links, like Tiger Woods and Phil Mickelson, who are able to earn tens of millions of dollars more than their opponents in tournament prizes and endorsements deals.

The difference between the best and the rest can be almost indiscernible to the untrained eye, but that slight edge can make the difference between mediocrity and incredible success.

If you want to make your way to the front of the pack, you need to look at your life and your business in a slightly different way than others do. Conventional *Blue Pill* viewpoints are not working for most people. If you think that you are going to be just fine during retirement because you are doing the same things financially that everyone else is doing, you may need to rethink your position. If everyone was right, then everyone would be rich.

Here are some very interesting numbers about retirement recently released from the U.S. Department of Health and Human Services, SSA Publication#13-11871[2]. For every 100 Americans born, upon reaching the retirement age of 65, here is what you will find:

- 25 will be dead;
- 49 will be dependent upon family or charity to maintain their standard of living or will still be working to make ends meet;
- 22 will have income below the poverty line;
- 4 will be financially independent.

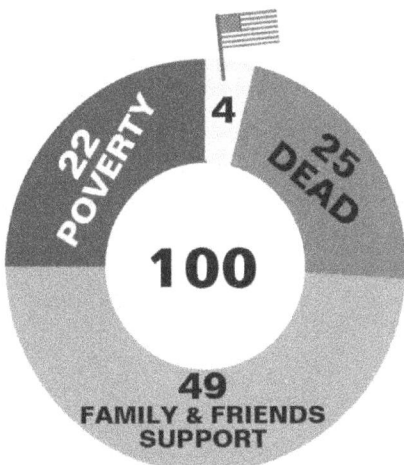

Now here is the shocking thing about these numbers. For most of the 96 out of 100 people who do not achieve financial independence, the reason is not because they did not earn enough money during their lifetime or acquire enough assets. Most people have earned plenty of money. The reason most are not financially independent is because they did not get *Right to the Money*. They did not protect their money, or they ignored some of the strategies outlined in this book. They have unknowingly and unnecessarily allowed great amounts of money to transfer from their own hands to big financial institutions, to the government or to Wall Street losses. They had plenty of seed corn, but they collected a tiny fraction of what they expected at harvest. Not because they didn't have the ability, but because they accepted some or all of the common conventional thinking as accurate; they took the Blue Pill.

Robert Ringer has a great deal of powerful life wisdom in his books, consulting, and on his website, www.RobertRinger.com. Here is what Robert Ringer says about conventional wisdom:

"I'd caution every investor to be very skeptical of conventional wisdom because not only is it often wrong, it's been my experience that quite often it's 180 degrees removed from the best course of action. Remember, conventional wisdom is not what moves civilization forward. Wisdom and progress are almost diametrically opposed. Progress results from the actions of a small minority of the earth's population that defies conventional wisdom. Just think about it for a second: Do the masses create any new products and services? No. They just sit on the sidelines and watch people with vision perform. And then, of course, once a new product or service is successful, they're more than happy to enjoy the fruits of the maverick's labor.

"As we all know, there's a strong instinct in human beings to follow the crowd, which is known in financial circles as the "lemming effect." I'm sure that all our listeners are familiar with this phenomenon — one person following another over the edge of a financial cliff. This phenomenon has been around since the beginning of recorded history. We saw it most recently in the dot-com implosion that devastated millions of investors beginning in the late 1990s [And

---

"To build a great company, which is a CEO's job, sometimes you have to stand up against conventional wisdom."
■ Carly Fiorina, former CEO Hewlett Packard

"Never accept ultimatums, conventional wisdom, or absolutes."
■ Christopher Reeves

"Common sense is not so common.
■ Voltaire

in the financial crisis of 2008-09]. But it's important to recognize that what's true for the lemming effect in the stock market is equally true in virtually all other areas of life. People have a natural desire to be on the side of popular opinion."[3]

Many people who have followed the conventional wisdom will end up with a fraction of the lifestyle they envisioned for themselves for retirement.

Align Your Sail to the Red Pill

We are living in absolutely incredible times. We are now in an era of high change, high opportunity, and high threat, all at the same time. There has always been change, opportunity and threats, but I believe there are two important differences now.

One, we live at a time that has a much greater *density* of opportunity and threat. More opportunity is available to more people than ever before. Most individuals can now pursue almost any opportunity they desire. It used to be that you had to have certain birthrights, connections, money, or secret methods or information to pursue certain opportunities. Today, if you are a self-starter, you can accomplish anything you desire.

Secondly, many of the threats to people's wealth are not clearly seen and understood by those taking the Blue Pill. In some instances, it is people following the conventional crowd view. In other cases, the view is distorted by the media by focusing attention on other things. In other cases the view may be filtered through a rose colored lens.

Today we have a very high rate of change and high degree of opportunity for those who know where to find it, how to access it and how to align with it. We have opportunities now that I could not have imagined as a boy growing up on a Minnesota farm in the early 70's. But, as the ups of the roller coaster go steeper and higher so do the downs go lower, faster, and deeper. We have more opportunities today than perhaps all of previous history combined. But we also have many huge minefields that we must sidestep in order to enjoy the fruits of today's opportunities. Most people will not be able to avoid all of the minefields because they are relying on a Blue Pill viewpoint to make decisions and take actions.

Imagine that we had a piece of land the size of a football field with thousands of 400-ounce bars of gold buried a few inches from the surface. And also buried, randomly intermingled amongst the gold bars and out of sight are hundreds of mines and bombs. What would you do? In my opinion, it would be extremely foolish to just barge in and begin extracting the gold bars. What if you saw other people walking in and starting to retrieve some of the gold bars? You might watch for a while but then after witnessing others getting some success without being blown up, you might begin to discount the danger of the bombs…..and then venture in yourself. Is this wise?

Following conventional wisdom along with the rest of the crowd is often the exact opposite from the best course of action. Probably not wise at all, especially if your goals have anything to do with long term wealth and health. You would likely get blown up by one of the bombs. Wouldn't it be better to know where the bombs are first? It would be even better if you also had a bomb diffuser and good protective gear. With this approach, you could then put on the protective gear, diffuse the bombs, and then retrieve the gold bars. Not being harmed would enable you to continue to build wealth -- without being harmed. Having the protective gear and the bomb diffuser are probably more important than attempting to build more wealth without any protection. What if you have already acquired such land that already has gold bars buried on it? You worked hard to acquire this wealth and you know precisely where you have placed these gold bars on the land.

You have a *Right to the Money*. But over time, bombs have found a way onto your land, some you may know about, others you may be unaware of. What if some of the unknown bombs are different? Instead of blowing up on contact, they instead silently release a virus that gradually kills you? In this situation, fewer people would even be aware enough to protect and grow their wealth.

In my opinion, the world we live in is much like this scenario. There are many, many gold bars of opportunity in today's world. But the threats to one's wealth in this world have also greatly increased. Some of these increased threats, although just as deadly, remain largely hidden out of sight from the masses. The nature of these *stealth* threats makes them more of a threat to your wealth than they need to be. Antidotes are available.

What are some of these threats?

Almost all western governments are caught between a rock and hard place – with no easy, politically acceptable solutions in sight. Technically many of these governments are bankrupt. There is far too much debt incurred by most Western governments. This debt is so large that one can only conclude it will not be paid back by the current generation in power. These debt problems have surfaced over the last several years, but the problems have not really been addressed. Kind of like spotting the tip of an iceberg breaking through the surface, and then pushing the iceberg back under the water so that it is out of sight. They have simply kicked the tin can down the road. Governments and central banks are attempting to gloss over these debts, and present the appearance of a returning prosperity. Prosperity is returning for some, but not all. Those that have the bomb diffusers, the protective gear, and the virus antidote are the ones who will have long lasting prosperity for themselves and their families.

Over the next several decades we will experience the greatest threats to wealth and its transfer in history.

> *"The conventional view serves to protect us from the painful job of thinking."*
>
> ~ John Kenneth Galbraith

Government debt ceiling and budget discussions, in my opinion, distort the real issue--what to do about the massive debt? Ultimately, if a compromise approach is used, it means taxes will go up AND entitlement programs like social security and Medicare benefits will go down? Looking at historical patterns, it is highly likely that both interest rates and inflation will go up in the future, maybe even dramatically. More outlays to pay increased taxes, more outlays for higher cost of living and less income for retirees from entitlement programs will push many of the "a little rich" back to middle class lifestyles. It will squeeze the unprepared middle class to lower middle class or poor lifestyles. Throw in a financial crisis every five to seven years and it will be a disaster for many of those that rely on the Blue Pill.

At the same time, there will also be individuals and families that will not only continue to prosper but will thrive in this environment. They took the Red Pill, made some tweaks to viewpoints and strategies, got a slight edge and will be much wealthier in the future than they are now.

In the tough environment in rural farming communities in the 1970's, I often heard people say, "the rich get richer and the poor get poorer." I think a more accurate view going forward would be *"those prepared properly – whether rich or poor -- will get richer. The unprepared –whether rich or poor -- will get poorer."*

Will you and your family be on the right side of these wealth transfers? Or will your wealth deplete like it will for many families?

The opportunities and threats, combined with aging baby boomer demographics are leading up to the *Greatest Wealth Transfer* in history. It is underway already. Which side will you and your family be on? Do you have a *Right to the Money*? I think you do.

"People think that at the top there isn't much room. They tend to think of it as an Everest. My message is that there is tons of room at the top."
~Margaret Thatcher

Chapter 2

Don't Lose Money

Now we come to what might seem like an elementary principle, but one that many people neglect nonetheless.

Investors both large and small risk their shirt in the publicly-traded financial markets because these markets offer a chance for them to risk it with the potential that if they make it, they could win big, very big. Unfortunately, most people lose their shirt in these markets rather than gaining huge profits.

The reason is simple: They approach the markets and investing with a gambling mentality instead of a wealth-building, compounding mentality. If you choose to compound your investments in the stock market, you better make sure you understand that you can lose it all quickly. The stock market has typically had a major downturn that can crush any investor about every five years, although in recent years it is proving to be even more volatile. Take a look at history and you will see that a major downturn approximately every five years has been the case. Sometimes it is a bit shorter than five years, sometimes a bit longer than five years. It has never been more than ten years between major downturns. Although it is still fresh in our minds, it has already been more than five years since the financial crisis of 2008.

Which brings me to the point of this chapter as we continue to consider the seven ways that wealthy investors expand their success: they don't lose money in huge amounts.

Think of Warren Buffett's famous two rules for investment success: *"Rule No. 1: never lose money; rule No. 2: don't forget rule No. 1"*

Unless you have prophetic powers, it will probably be impossible for you to never lose money, and I think even Buffett understands that. Buffett has had investments that did not work out. However, you can and should develop a strategy and attitude, a mindset that will enable you to limit your losses and limit them quickly. If you have a small fire that accidently starts in your home, you obviously want to get that fire out immediately – while it is still small and containable. A small fire put out quickly, while certainly not a pleasant experience, is not catastrophic if dealt with quickly. You should have the same urgency with investment losses. Stop them before they become catastrophic. This chapter will give a brief overview of how to restrict your losses.

Consider the numbers in the table below. *Table 1* shows the rate of return required after you suffer a loss, just to get back to break-even status:

Table 1

Amount of Loss	Return Needed to Get to Break-Even
10%	11.1%
20%	25%
30%	70%
50%	100%
70%	333%

Those numbers are stunning, aren't they? These numbers are why you should never tolerate a 20 percent loss or shrug your shoulders over a 30 percent loss. The gains you will need to make to counter-balance those losses are formidable, and the chances of you picking the right stocks to make up that kind of ground are slim.

My fundamental point is to **never let a small loss turn into a huge loss.** If you are invested in the stock market, what do you think is the chance of having a 30or 50 percent loss? It's much higher than most people think, especially in light of the recent market crises of 2002 and 2008-09, when many investments suffered 30 to 50 percent losses—or more. If you suffered that kind of downturn, what would be the likelihood of your investment rebounding by 70 percent just to get to break-even? And why waste four or five years of dead money to maybe get back to even? You are skilled enough in math to know that such a winner stock profile is unlikely.

The prominent financial research firm Dalbar has done many studies on investor behavior and their results, and they discover the same patterns again and again—most investors sell at the bottom and buy at the top. As a result, they often earn less than 2 percent on average on their very risky investments, even when the markets have done much better.[iv] The difference between these two levels of performance is called a "Behavior Gap," and I am determined to combat that in this book.

Part of the reason for this "Behavior Gap," I believe, is the common wisdom that favors a "buy-and-hold" mentality championed by most sources of "conventional wisdom". This premise assumes that the stock market is like a cash machine that dispenses cash without debiting your account. The thinking is that if you stand at the machine long enough, you will get rich, no brains required.

And what if the cash machine malfunctions? No problem, it will soon be repaired. Consequently, the best advice is to stay in line even when the machine is not working well. That way, you will be ready to collect your money when it's up and running again. This is "buy-and-hold" in a nutshell and it might have worked in other eras, but most cutting-edge financial advisors believe that its day has passed for a long list of reasons.

"Buy-and-hold" is still the precious tenet that most investors hold today, especially those who have been in the game for a long time. This mentality steers the decisions of millions of people and undergirds most of the financial industry— that the ATM will right itself, given enough time. For that reason, the investor should just be patient and take an extremely long-term view.

Proponents of "buy-and-hold" say that their approach is reinforced by experience, especially recent experience. Much of the last three decades of market history provides no convincing counter-example, they claim. Stock prices will eventually go up, given enough time.

This, we believe, can be a very dangerous view for you to take as an investor.

For one thing, many trusted voices who analyze the markets believe that "Buy-and-hold" is largely dead as a strategy. Andrew Lo, the well-respected finance professor at MIT's Sloan School of Management, offers this comment in a recent interview:

"Buy-and-hold doesn't work anymore. The volatility is too significant. Almost any asset can suddenly become much more risky. Buying into a mutual fund and holding it for 10 years is no longer going to deliver the same kind of expected return that we saw over the course of the last seven decades, simply because of the nature of financial markets and how complex it's gotten."[v]

Lo is not alone in that opinion. Daryl Guppy, a CNBC contributor on finance, offers excellent hard evidence in a recent post entitled "Long-Term Investing is Dead; Check the S&P Chart." His conclusion after an analysis of the S&P 500 Monthly Chart over the past 15 years?

"The message is clear. The money comes from trading the rally uptrends. It's also made trading short on the retreats. You do not have to buy exact tops and bottoms to make a better return. Returns on capital from investing do not come from buy-and-hold."[vi]

Fabrice Taylor, a prominent Canadian financial journalist chimes in as part of his recent "Don't Believe Buffett—Buy-and-hold Investing is Dead" article, stating that technology has eroded many trusted brands that could be invested in and relied upon to return a solid investment over many years. Taylor mentions Western Union, Eastman Kodak and toy companies as examples of solid enterprises that have had their markets eroded or destroyed by new tech companies. As a result, there are fewer and fewer blue-chip companies to invest in and to apply a buy-and-hold strategy.[vii]

Because of the newly discovered holes in the buy-and-hold approach, we recommend a few strategies to protect your money from large losses in the markets. One easy way to do that is to pull a portion of your money out of the markets and pour it into collateral-based hard assets. These holdings, such as real estate or loans backed by a large equity cushion of real estate, can protect you from wild plunges in the market, which have been more frequent in recent years.

True, real estate has had its tough times in the past decade, obviously, but if you shop carefully, and manage property professionally, you can stay out of the huge-loss category. The same goes for well-selected multi-family apartments, trophy properties, and select energy markets—they rarely plunge to the lows that the financial markets do, thus enabling you to control the exposure of your money and not lose it in large quantities.

For the rest of your money that remains wrapped up in the markets, don't be fearful. Using wisdom as you invest can earn you money and keep you away from painful losses. To keep it simple, **realize that there are two kinds of investors in the world – investors who will cut their losses and those who won't.** As all of the research shows, the latter group is larger, much larger. This bunch rode the market up in the late 1990s, and they rode it all the way down in 2000, 2001, and 2002. Then, even if they recovered part of their losses over the next four years, they rode it all the way back down again in 2008 and early 2009. Were you in that group? I certainly hope not! If so, you've come to the right book for better ideas.

What are the reasons for this nettlesome "behavior gap" that investors have, where they are almost destined to buy high and sell low? I believe one huge reason that is not discussed often enough is that staying with a stock becomes a matter of pride and a weird sort of masculinity. Investors who ride out the storms all the way to the bottom of the ocean make statements such as, *"I am not a quitter. I can handle the price going down."*

That is true to a degree; if you choose to invest in the stock market, you know that losses are part of the adventure. If those losses stay small, they don't hurt too much, and are easily offset by the winning investments in your portfolio. Inexperienced investors often see even small losses as failures and direct attacks on their intellect. I want to change your entire mind-set about these small losses, however. It's time to start seeing them as victories—**victories against big losses, which must be avoided at all costs**. No one can afford a big loss if all of his or her money is in the stock market.

As one wise person once said: *"The problem is: you only have to be wrong once to suffer a catastrophic loss."*

This chapter is written to help protect you from such a catastrophe.

If investors could just learn one secret, it would be to cut your loser investments short and let your winners run. Do everything possible to keep from incurring large losses. If you don't take these two bits of advice, you may *never* be successful as an investor.

No one, not even Warren Buffett, gets every investment right. I don't get every investment right. You will not, either. When you do make a mistake and pick a loser, you need to admit it right away and move on. When you pick a winner, hold onto it as long as possible.

These maxims sound so easy and self-evident that you might question their value, but every piece of research shows that investors have an extremely difficult time cutting losers and riding winners. In fact, many investors do just the opposite—they sell their winners to chalk up some quick gains and hold onto their losers in hopes that they will rebound. Legendary portfolio manager Peter Lynch addressed that in his best-seller, One Up on Wall Street: *"Selling your winners and holding your losers,"* he said, *"is like cutting your flowers and watering your weeds."*

One group of investors that I find has a particularly tough time applying these simple approaches are those with an impressive résumé full of formal education. Because of their long list of degrees from prestigious schools, many of these well-educated investors often think that they are smarter than the market. That pride can run so deep as to astonish you. Joe Harvard Grad emerges from Business School with his M.B.A. and says to himself: *"I will out-smart the market and make millions."*

Yet, even if Mr. Harvard Grad is right most of the time, almost all of the time, it will only take one giant loss to ruin his fortune. And here's news brief: *everyone* is wrong at least once every few years.

Consequently, you must rule out the possibility by being a disciplined investor and not riding out losers. You MUST cut your losses and let your winners run until they tire.

Need I point out how especially important it is to not lose money to people who are nearing retirement? A huge loss in the market can force you back to work, out of your home or into a less desirable retirement community, among other consequences. For those who are nearing or have reached retirement age, it can be a matter of having a great future or living in poverty. So cut losses quickly and never, ever let a small loss turn into a large loss.

Other seemingly small ways to prepare for retirement or live comfortably during those years would include:

- Becoming more tax-efficient and getting the maximum tax refund each year as you double-check all of your possible tax breaks, deductions and credits

- Choosing investments that slant the risk-reward ratio in your favor

- Being aware of the significant conflicts of interest that can exist between investment banks and brokerage houses with investors. In one case, I saw a Wall Street institution program that had numerous fees totaling 32 percent. Investors in that program were immediately behind the eight ball, and did not have a large probability of success in that program.

- Restructuring your mortgage if necessary to build wealth safely

- Maximizing net spendable retirement income by making sure you have a certain level of liquid assets that can be easily cashed in.

- Have at least some of your income be legally tax free.

All of these are easy, quick steps that can add up to a significant change in your retirement income and cash flow.

As you take these steps, don't bail out on the stock market altogether. As you move forward, invest wisely and vow to not live out the "behavior gap" as you cut losses swiftly. Consider these concluding steps to build wealth:

1. Diversify a portion of your wealth into physical, hard asset investments such as trophy properties that produce rental income or some form of cash flow, maybe royalties or business operating income.

2. For the portion of your wealth that you do keep in the stock market, find ways to reduce or manage that risk. Set trailing stop-loss strategies so that your maximum loss on any investment is not <u>ever</u>

more than 20 to 25 percent. Some investors use even tighter stops of 8 to 10 percent. For example, everything else being equal, someone approaching retirement could conclude that they need a tighter stop loss provision than someone just launching their career. There certainly are situations for some investors where the stock market is not appropriate at all. All that you need to do to safeguard yourself in this way is to decide at the time of investment what the maximum loss is that you are willing to risk on a single investment.

As this chapter with the simple maxim of "Don't Lose Money" concludes, remember that the most perfect investment in the world would have three characteristics:

1. It would have a good rate of return.
2. It would be safe, with no or low risk.
3. You would be able to liquidate it immediately.

Now, let me ask you: What investment has all three of those characteristics?

The answer is: none.

Such an investment does not exist.

Now what?

I would say that with a little effort, you can find investments that have two of the three characteristics listed above. You don't want to be like the investors who don't have *any* of these three qualities in their investments. They invest where there is little or no return, massive risk, and their money is tied up for a very long period of time. Stay out of that camp!

A reasonable approach would be to pick an investment with any two of the three features, for example the stock market, which has the potential for a good return and is generally liquid. The market, however, is not a no-risk investment.

Similarly, cash in the bank is generally considered no-risk (up to FDIC limits) and it is liquid, but it does not earn a good return. In fact, cash has a *negative* real return now when you factor in true inflation.

Perhaps you could allocate a portion of your portfolio to investments that have a good return potential and relatively safe, no or low-risk profiles. Would it be worth it to you to give up some immediate liquidity on some of your money? A segment of your wealth could be tied up for two, four or seven years. It should be noted that most billionaires and mega-millionaires operate in this way. They have a substantial portion of their wealth tied up in businesses, real estate, fine art, or other assets that are not quickly able to be turned into cash. To obtain meaningful growth in your portfolio – wealth that can span generations – diversify it and be patient with your investments, but not overly patient with the money that you have in the market. In that case, as I hope that I have been clear, stop the bleeding as soon as you can.

Cut your losses quickly, eliminate the "behavior gap" and your gains should outweigh your losses nicely. Don't lose money in large quantities.

It's that simple, and that difficult.

If it were easy, everyone would do it.

Just as one shoe may not be a fit for everyone, one strategy to Don't Lose Money may not be the best fit for all investors. Sometimes, we don't know what we don't know. Did you know there is another Don't Lose Money strategy and it also has dramatic tax benefits, far surpassing the small tax benefits you may receive from 401Ks, IRAs or Roth accounts?

To read this bonus chapter, go to:

www.RighToTheMoney.com/SpecialBonus1

"An investment in knowledge pays the best interest."
                                                    ~ Benjamin Franklin

Chapter 3

The Eighth Wonder of the World

Compound interest is one of the greatest wonders ever discovered by humans. It has been called the eighth wonder of the world by the likes of Baron Rothschild, Ben Franklin, and Albert Einstein. Einstein further stated that *"compounding is mankind's greatest invention because it allows for the reliable, systematic accumulation of wealth."*

All great investors understand the power of compounding and put that concept to work for the benefit of themselves and their families. To ensure a consistent and long term *Right to the Money* this strategy is absolutely essential. It is the power of small things adding up. Small amounts of money reinvested over time can build a substantial fortune. Small habits compounded over time can have geometric impacts. Most people understand compound interest at an intellectual level, but few of those decide to act and put this simple and powerful tool into play.

> *"Compound interest is the eighth wonder of the world. He who understands it, earns it ... he who doesn't ... pays it."*
> ~ Albert Einstein

Richard Russell of the Dow Theory Letters eloquently presents the power of compound interest. I highly recommend that you read and subscribe to Richard Russell's Dow Theory Letters[viii]. Mr. Russell says:

"Compounding is the royal road to riches. Compounding is the safe road, the sure road, and, fortunately, anybody can do it. To compound successfully you need the following: perseverance, intelligence and knowledge.

Perseverance will keep you firmly on the savings [investing] path. You need intelligence in order to understand what you are doing and why. And you need knowledge of the simple mathematics in order to comprehend the amazing power that will come to you if you faithfully follow the compounding road. And, of course, you need time to allow the power of compounding to work for you. It is very important to understand this principle: compounding only works through time.

But there are two catches in the compounding process. The first is obvious – compounding may involve sacrifice (you can't both spend a dollar and still save that dollar). Second, compounding is boring–b-o-r-i-n-g. Or I should say, it's boring until after seven or eight years when the money starts to pour in. Then, believe me, compounding becomes very interesting. In fact, it becomes downright fascinating! When you plant a garden, the first few weeks can be boring, but the growth of the garden accelerates once the roots have firmly established themselves."

"A penny saved is a penny earned."
~ Benjamin Franklin

In order to truly appreciate the power of compounding, I am including this extraordinary comparison in Table 2. In this comparison, we assume that investor Sally opens an IRA at age 20. For seven consecutive years she puts $5,000 into her IRA at an average return rate of 10 percent (7 percent interest plus growth). After seven years she makes *no more* contributions--she's finished. A second investor, Tom, makes no contributions until age 27 (this is the age when Sally was finished with her contributions). Then Tom continues faithfully to contribute $5,000 every year until he's 65 (at the same theoretical 10 percent rate).

Table 2. Hypothetical example.

	Investor Tom			Investor Sally	
Age	Contribution	Year End Value		Contribution	Year End Value
20	$0			$5,000	$5,500
21	$0			$5,000	$11,550
22	$0			$5,000	$18,205
23	$0			$5,000	$25,526
24	$0			$5,000	$33,578
25	$0			$5,000	$42,436
26	$0			$5,000	$52,179
27	$5,000	$5,500		$5,000	$62,897
28	$5,000	$11,550			$69,187
29	$5,000	$18,205			$76,106
30	$5,000	$25,526			$83,716
31	$5,000	$33,578			$92,088
32	$5,000	$42,436			$101,297
33	$5,000	$52,179			$111,427
34	$5,000	$62,897			$122,569
35	$5,000	$74,687			$134,826
36	$5,000	$87,656			$148,309
37	$5,000	$101,921			$163,140
38	$5,000	$117,614			$179,454
39	$5,000	$134,875			$197,399
40	$5,000	$153,862			$217,139
41	$5,000	$174,749			$238,853
42	$5,000	$197,724			$262,738
43	$5,000	$222,996			$289,012
44	$5,000	$250,795			$317,913
45	$5,000	$281,375			$349,704
46	$5,000	$315,012			$384,675
47	$5,000	$352,014			$423,142
48	$5,000	$392,715			$465,456
49	$5,000	$437,487			$512,002
50	$5,000	$486,735			$563,202
51	$5,000	$540,909			$619,522
52	$5,000	$600,500			$681,475
53	$5,000	$666,050			$749,622
54	$5,000	$738,155			$824,584
55	$5,000	$817,470			$907,043
56	$5,000	$904,717			$997,747
57	$5,000	$1,000,689			$1,097,522
58	$5,000	$1,106,258			$1,207,274
59	$5,000	$1,222,383			$1,328,001
60	$5,000	$1,350,122			$1,460,801
61	$5,000	$1,490,634			$1,606,882
62	$5,000	$1,645,197			$1,767,570
63	$5,000	$1,815,217			$1,944,327
64	$5,000	$2,002,239			$2,138,759
65	$5,000	**$2,207,963**			**$2,352,635**

Now study the incredible results! Sally, who made her contributions earlier and who made only eight contributions, ends up with *more* money than Tom, who made 39 contributions but at a *later time*. The difference in the two is that *Sally had seven more early years of compounding than Tom.* Those seven early years were worth more than all of Tom's 32 additional contributions.

"This is a comparison that I suggest you show to your kids. It's a study I've lived by, and I can tell you, it works."

There are several ways to harness and even magnify the power of compound interest. Time is the great advantage. Start the habit as early as you can even if the amounts are smaller.

Reinvest all of the earnings/gain that you can. In the first 10 years of my own investing with alternative assets, I did not withdraw any earnings. In fact, since the beginning we have managed cash flow very frugally by keeping tight controls on costs. Money was spent only when absolutely necessary.

This allows one to compound even more earnings back directly back into investments. I have seen too many investors who withdraw and spend their earnings as soon as they earn a nice return. They take the profit and spend it to celebrate their good fortune. But this is like pulling up the seedlings that were just planted before they have been able to produce a harvest.

A variation of this that was often said in farming communities like the one where I grew up, *"Don't eat your seed corn."* It is better to do whatever you have to do so that you can keep the earnings compounding as long as possible before you start taking the harvest.

If it means living frugally until you get the compounding pump primed, then live frugally. Position yourself to benefit from the power of compounding. Live frugally, if needed. Don't eat your seed corn, nor should you pull the corn plant out of the ground just after it has sprouted roots.

Compounding Club

There are many investments that can fit into the Compounding Club. Some of these investments will allow you to automatically re-invest the earnings. But for those that don't, you can steer the earnings to a cash accumulation account and then use that cash to buy another Compounding Club investment.

These can be investments that pay steady payments from blue chip companies. Make sure these are blue chip companies today; many blue chip companies of the past are no longer "blue chips" as their brands and profit margins have eroded because of technological advances. Think Kodak.

Besides bonds on blue chip companies, you could also buy dividend paying stocks of blue chip companies. I recommend that you look for companies that display behaviors and actions where the company management actually has a demonstrated track record of doing things that are in the best interest of investors. Here are some behavior examples I like to see:

- Companies that buy back their own shares
- Companies with a long history of paying *increasing* dividends,
- Companies that own or control strong brands in their marketplace
- Companies where key executives act like owners and preferably are also stockholders.

True Asset Allocation

I also believe that for many it is prudent to add certain alternative investments to your Compounding Club portfolio. We use an investment formula that won Dr. Harold Markowitz the Nobel Prize in finance in 1990. His approach demonstrates how you can maximize your profits and minimize your risk by properly allocating assets and rebalancing your portfolio. The publication of Dr. Markowitz's theories gave the terms "asset allocation" and "diversification" a great deal of attention.

Unfortunately, much of Wall Street then used this idea to sell more securities to the public by using the terms "asset allocation" and "diversification" *without really following Dr. Markowitz's formula.*

The best application of asset allocation means spreading investments across truly different asset classes, not just across a few mutual funds or stocks and bonds. Buying three, four or five different stocks or mutual funds is not true asset class diversification. Asset allocation refers to spreading your investments among different asset classes, not just different securities or market sectors. Doing this has allowed some investors to prosper and thrive during the longest bear market since The Great Depression. The best have had money invested in recent years in alternative investments not correlated to the stock market. Many times, while the stock market has gone down, these have produced steady dividends or interest or rental income or distribution checks.

Money can be invested in niche hard asset investments. They have also generally given us a positive return in a catastrophic environment. The same is true with collateralized notes, equipment leasing, energy programs, precious metals, and other high yield investments. Because different asset classes are imperfectly correlated – some zig while others zag– this approach allows you to boost returns while reducing your portfolio's volatility.

True asset allocation should be the foundation of your entire investment strategy. It's critical to your long-term financial health, and they can be great inflation hedges.

Where are interest rates now? They are at historical lows and are much more likely to go up than further down. What happens to a long-term bond portfolio when interest rates go up? Generally, when interest rates go up, the value of a long-term bond portfolio will drop. To benefit from this you have to adjust your portfolio **before** rates go up.

My favorite alternative investments that can fit into the Compounding Club include[ix]:

- Tax lien investing
- Hard money lending well secured by real estate

- Bridge financing to small businesses well secured by assets of the business, such as inventory, accounts receivable, and real estate
- Energy and resource based royalties. These companies include groups of intelligent mining insiders that bring their capital and invest in projects. They have many benefits. They don't drill or explore. Instead, they make calculated bets on projects they trust. Most good royalty companies are run by insiders in the resource and mining area. They know the best projects and have the best management teams. They often have a lower risk way to make big gains.
- Well purchased cash flow single family rental properties
- Well purchased multi-family apartments

Avoid Headaches and Reduce Risk

Diversify across multiple compounding investments or deals. Don't have all your eggs in one basket. If you want to allocate $500,000 to hard asset investments, like bridge loans, it is better to have five $100,000 loans than a single loan for $500,000.

After you have a few hard asset compounding investments in place, consider diversifying also to different locations; e.g., if all of your collateralized loans were done on properties in Las Vegas, which experienced an extreme 50 percent decreases in value during the financial crisis– that is not good. Better to spread your money across multiple geographies and multiple types of deals. Look for locations that have solid economies that are more resilient to recession and have good prospects for long term growth. While no one can predict the future, I like areas with good job growth, population growth, and comfortable climates. For example, I have found that neighborhoods with increasing elementary school enrollments can be a decent predictor of future above-average home price increases.

Instead of doing all the work yourself, partner with an expert in a particular area first. Find a partner who is experienced in that area. Let them do the work while you put up the money, or some combination of tasks and money investment that works for all involved. Bet on the partner with the winning track record.

Otherwise you will pay tuition for someone less experienced to learn the successful methods.

Build and use the A Team to reduce headaches. For example, when I started at around age 25, I did all of the property management myself, but not because I loved screening tenants, doing repairs, or collecting rent. At the time, I did it to save money. I soon learned that it made more sense to have someone else handle the property management duties, *especially if the game is something that you want to play for the long term.* There is more money to be made in the deal making and investing portion, less to be made in property management. Nothing wrong if you choose to do the property managing yourself, but if you do not enjoy it, I would strongly suggest getting it outsourced to someone else. After a while many people realize their time is better spent on deal-making than on property management. If you choose to do the property management yourself because outsourcing is too expensive, then you need to restructure your deals so there is plenty of cash flow in the deal to handle property management expenses. More on A-Team talent later.

Ditto on outsourcing daily operations. If you decide to not take a two-week ski vacation to Colorado because you are too busy running day to day tasks on a property or business, you need to restructure your deals or choose different types of deals. In my opinion, you should choose deals that enhance rather than downgrade your lifestyle.

Compounding is a Get Richer Slowly strategy. Throughout the years, I have seen the following situation taking place. If an investor expects to make a lot of money quickly, more often than not, they end up losing. If they expect to make a little at a time, as with a compounding strategy, they typically make a lot in the long run.

What do experienced, successful investors do? They combine compounding strategies with steady investments that possess a higher degree of wealth preservation – often times with investments backed by hard assets.

How long does it take to double your money using compounding? If the returns are reinvested consistently at the same rate of return, you can use the Rule of 72 to estimate the time it takes to double your money. The rule of 72 is to divide the rate of return into the number 72; the result is the numbers of years it will take to double your money. For example, if you have an investment that pays 7.2 percent each year and you reinvest the earnings in that investment, and then divide 7.2 into 72, the result is that your money will double in 10 years. If you earn 10 percent per year, your money will double in 7.2 years.

Learn how to make hard money private loans for rehab projects that are well secured by real estate. Follow this link for a bonus chapter that shows you how:

www.RightToTheMoney.com/SpecialReport2.

Those who apply compound interest earn interest. Those who don't apply compound interest end up paying interest.

Earning interest instead of paying interest is a key hallmark of an investor who has a *Right to the Money*.

Chapter 4

Get Your Home Work Done

Due diligence and the importance of doing your homework

In high school and college, if you wanted to succeed, it was important to do your homework. It was the great equalizer. A kid of average talent could surpass a kid of greater talent just by working harder on his homework. The students who did the most homework were usually the ones who had the greatest academic success.

The same can be said for investing. Just don't let the dog eat your homework. There's no excuse—not even your dog—for not doing your homework when it's your money at stake. But unlike high school, in the world of investing, you can enlist a team of qualified experts to do much of the homework for you. You can have your lawyer, your CPA, your realtor, or your appraiser, and other experts weigh-in and handle key parts of your homework.

When you're dealing with complex investments such as bridge loans and other investments that we discussed as part of the Compound Interest Club, you really do need the help of financial specialists to handle most of your homework for you. Even though you are ultimately the one responsible for getting your homework done, it has been my experience that most successful investors are wise enough to understand their limitations and bring in some experts to handle the part of the homework they're not qualified to do, or do not want to do.

Having said that, it is also important to maintain balance. You may have heard the old adage that most attorneys are deal killers—and of course, some deals should be killed. But don't let an attorney make your decisions for you. A good attorney should be able to provide counsel, state the pros and cons and offer his or her opinion, but the final decision is in your hands.

Another benefit a good attorney can bring to the table is suggesting ways to restructure a deal to make it worth doing. For example, let's suppose you were making a hard money loan, secured by real estate as collateral. The appraisal and repair estimates both came back and there was not enough equity cushion in the real estate to justify the risk. If other parameters are good, an investor might return to the would-be borrower and get additional collateral from other real estate properties or other assets to also be pledged as collateral to sweeten the deal enough to make it work.

Due Diligence the Right Way

The Harvard Business Review states, *"Deal making is glamorous; due diligence is not."* But it is the right execution of due diligence – doing the homework –that determines if a potential investment should be pursued, restructured or abandoned altogether.

It's a lack of due diligence that has led many people to make investments that have added little value to their portfolios. Don't get me wrong, there are many good due diligence resources around, but all too often it's hard to walk away from a deal that has momentum once you have aligned yourself with the deal.

The problem is, after managers have put in the time and effort to do their due diligence and hammer together an agreement, they feel like they have too much invested to walk away—even if the deal is deeply flawed. And the closer to completion the deal gets, the more difficult it becomes to make the decision to kill it. Momentum can be a driving factor for both the individual making a small acquisition or a lender making a hard money real estate loan.

Homework

1. .... ☑
2. .... ☑
3. .... ☑
4. .... ☐
5. .... ☐

But to continue to pursue a flawed deal just because you have too much time and energy tied up in it to walk away essentially defeats the whole purpose of due diligence. The main reason you do your homework is to decide whether or not the deal is worth doing. If your findings suggest that it isn't, you need to be prepared to walk away, confident that your efforts represented time well spent by identifying a deal that wasn't going to work. As Donald Trump said, *"sometimes the best investments are the ones you don't make."*

But conducting proper due diligence can also help you identify areas that could be modified to make a deal more plausible, more profitable, AND less risky. If you can figure out how to squeeze out the risk or restructure the deal to minimize the risk, you may be able to keep the deal on track.

When you do your homework correctly, it can either dramatically deepen your conviction about proceeding with the investment or save you a large amount of money by changing your mind, said Brad Henderson, managing director of The Boston Consulting Group.

In my opinion, most "due diligence" processes could be dramatically improved by shifting the focus away from simply verifying financial information and more toward developing a business plan to create, unlock, or realize value.

Even the term itself, *due diligence*, implies checking out the facts, verifying data. But in my opinion, this type of due diligence is only the first step. A good due diligence process should also develop a value projection based on various "what-if" scenarios of the future.

Due diligence should be used to test the business model in light of strengths and weaknesses. To be fair, some investors have an additional step (sometimes referred to as a "deal analysis") that follows the initial due diligence stage.

Thorough due diligence is vital because no one lives in a static world. Sometimes, for one plus one to equal two, you have to be very sure that each "one" is really a "one," not a phantom "one." After this baseline has been verified, then you can explore synergies where the business model or "what-if" factors can be synergistic–where one plus one can equal three.

Quantity or Quality?

Finding good deals is also a numbers game. In my experience, I might look at dozens of potential deals, quickly filter the list down to 10, and then select three for deeper homework. From those final three, I'll choose the one that looks the best.

About 25 years ago, I heard a speaker named Ron LeGrand. He had a lot of great ideas, but he said one thing that has proven itself many times over since I had first heard Ron say it:

> *"Some will. Some won't. So what? Next."*

There are many great deals to be found, created, and structured. Choose the best ones to move forward with. That one word "next," in and of itself, will give you an incredible amount of power if you have the discipline to use it. It means having the discipline to walk away from a deal that is not good enough or has too many risks that can't be successfully managed. When your homework exposes unfixable weaknesses in the deals you're considering, your decision should be a very simple one: Next!

It is best to concentrate your efforts on finding a few makeable deals rather than working on a large number of questionable deals and clinging to a desperate hope that one of them will miraculously close.

Successful investment in hard asset investments or bridge loans requires that you understand four crucial factors:

1. **What exactly is being acquired or pledged as collateral?** Is it the real estate? The business on the real estate? The cash flow? The natural resource or mineral deposits below ground? Or is one or more of these items being used to secure a bridge loan?

2. **What other liabilities come with the asset?** When he was Secretary of Defense under President George W. Bush, Donald Rumsfeld once said: *"There are known knowns. These are things we know that we know. There are unknowns. That is to say, there are things that we know we don't know. But there are also unknown unknowns. These are things we don't*

know we don't know. "When you're doing your due diligence, you need to make sure you answer every question so that there are as few "unknown unknowns" in the deal as possible. Otherwise you could be in for a very unpleasant surprise. I knew an investor who made a commercial acquisition and believed all of the debts on the property were revealed on the title report. But in that specific legal jurisdiction, unpaid utilities bills—even though not recorded—were attached to the property whether the buyer was aware of them or not.

3.   **What is the intrinsic value of the asset given its liabilities and current situation?** It is best to develop a range of intrinsic values for each property given the variation in the current environment.

4.   **What can be done to increase intrinsic value and reduce or eliminate liabilities?** Is the new business model's cashflow machine sustainable? What must be re-invested to keep it sustainable? Is the business model scalable?

The Importance of Talent

One of the most important elements in putting a deal together is to be sure you're working with a highly talented team of individuals. Bring the A team, because the more qualified your talent, the more smoothly the deal will evolve. If it is a significant investment, you may even want a Dream Team[x] of the best of the best, most qualified individuals for that industry.

I prefer to partner with others who are trustworthy and A-team competent to run the day-to-day operations.

If you are considering a deal that already has a team in place, compare them to your A team. The person running the day-to-day operation of a deal (I call that person my potential "operating partner"), should be an Olympic-caliber A team player.

You need to find out their level of relevant experience. By experience, I mean what is their experience relative to key skills needed for success? For instance, if you are providing a bridge loan for 16 percent plus four origination points and the loan proceeds are planned for acquisition and property rehabilitation, you need to know if the borrower has experience in property rehab or if someone on her team has experience with rehab projects. If she has done more than 50 rehab projects, I would be comfortable with her experience. If it is her first one, I would probably insist that she get an experienced, qualified rehabber on her team first. My point is that *the experience has to be relevant to the key skills needed for project success.*

Doug Casey of Casey Research is one of the best hard asset investors in the world. I highly recommend his books, products, and services. Here is what Doug says about people:

"The first question you want answered iswho are the key players involved with the company?' As is the case with all human beings, some are more skilled, more honest and harder working than others. To state the obvious, Boy Scout virtues like honesty, thrift, courage, and diligence are always good traits for your management teams, as are competence, knowledge, experience and, perhaps most importantly, a track record of success. You can find this information from a variety of sources, starting with management biographies (increasingly available on company web sites), then doing your research by talking with the managers themselves or their investor relations staff...... And don't hesitate to ask your broker or even competitors what they think about the people in the deal. Despite being a multi-billion-dollar, global business, the mining and resource industry is actually a pretty small village. If someone is a known snake oil salesman or poseur, chances are good you'll be able to ferret out that fact with just a couple of phone calls.

"In addition to trying to sort out the black hats, a key goal of this exercise is to find out if investors have made money in their past deals. Or, if things didn't work out too well — mining is a high-risk business, after all — did the company at least make an honest attempt to 'do the right thing' for their shareholders?

Remember, nothing succeeds like success... As someone who habitually looks for the opportunity embedded in just about any crisis, we use the labor shortage as a useful leading indicator by watching the career moves of the superstar mining pros. The good ones are in such demand that they can work for pretty much any company they want to... and so, as is human nature, gravitate to those projects which they believe will provide them with the best personal upside. Conversely, if the good people start to jump ship from a company, it may be a negative indicator. In the final analysis — bet on the winners."

Although Casey is referring to mining investments, his approach and attitude can be scaled and applied to any hard asset project.

The talent and energy of the human(s) running your project is the single most important factor in almost every project. A talented person can make lemonade when the lemons of the deal are revealed. A person with poor talent can screw up even an easy, straight-forward project. When things get tough on a project, you will be glad you have the A team.

Human talent is even more important when acquiring a business. Tom Shahnazarian, CEO of Spectrum Search Partners, finds the top talent in the world for private equity firms when a new CEO or COO is needed to run a turn-around situation or launch a new business model. Tom has told me more than once, in summary: *"Having top human talent counts the most when a business needs a turn-around or is about to take a business to another level. For a business that is coasting, only average talent may be needed; for a business that is game-changing, top talent is absolutely key."*

It is especially important to include the A team in the deal performance incentives so that if certain performance measures and deadlines are met or exceeded, they can earn additional benefits. For those incentives to have a meaningful impact on effort and performance, they should be explained and re-emphasized on an ongoing basis. I discuss the importance of human talent much more in the chapter on "Relational Capital."

When you have capital and talent, then at certain times in the business cycle you can get great trophy assets at great prices and make great profits. Your talent must have the patience and intestinal fortitude to get the timing mostly correct.

> *"The most effective [private equity directors] make a real effort to build a relationship of trust with management and actively use their skills, knowledge, and network of contacts."*
>
> ~ Working with Private Equity Portfolio Companies, January 2013 KPMG

Key Elements of the Screening Process

Working with great talent is probably the most important element of the screening process, but there are several other factors you also need to consider in every deal you investigate. The screening process can be fairly straight-forward if you know exactly what areas you need to investigate. In addition to making sure you have A-level talent, here are the other keys to a successful deal screening process:

Property. You need a thorough understanding of the property that is being acquired. What asset, exactly, is being acquired or pledged as collateral? What about the real estate? The business on the real estate? The cash flow? The natural resource or mineral deposits below ground? If it is a commercial property, are the air rights above the property included? If it is a land development deal, are water rights included or is water access available easily year round? Is one or more of these items used as collateral to secure a bridge loan? You also need to determine the current "as-is" value. For a property that is in need of rehab, you need to know what its true worth is *in the current market environment under its current use.* I once reviewed a property that was, in reality, worth less than the value of the land that the property stood on. The property was massively out of code and outdated. The cheapest way to turn around that property would have been to bulldoze the structure and start over from scratch. The want-to-be seller should have subtracted the cost of bulldozing from the market value of the land to determine the real value.

Unless you are an expert in valuation of the target asset, I would recommend that you appoint an experienced appraiser to handle the valuation. To protect yourself, I also recommend obtaining an independent Broker's Price Opinion (BPO) to validate the information from the formal appraisal. This may be less important now, post-crisis with new stricter appraisal guidelines in place. But during the hyperactive, hyperbolic, pre-bubble-burst parts of the business cycle, you would have been very wise to obtain an independent BPO to validate the value. On the other hand, after you have done many other deals in that same neighborhood, then an appraisal from a good licensed and experienced appraiser is probably sufficient. As you do more deals in a specific location, you will develop a good sense of the market and of values.

Appraisals today are much closer to value truth than they were in 2006 and 2007. Sometimes when I am weeding through potential deals, I get a BPO from a realtor who is experienced and knows that neighborhood well. I also like to have the appraiser and realtor estimate the value "after-repaired" or after the asset is improved, or re-positioned to a better, more profitable use, or modernized. This "to-be" value estimate should be produced by an expert using conservative assumptions.

Both an appraiser and a realtor will use comparable recently sold properties in the area to determine value of your target property. Another important piece of information to learn--in my opinion--is the Average Days on Market for that specific neighborhood. This is an indication of how quickly properties in that area are selling. I consider 60 or fewer Average Days on Market to be very good. If the area has a very high Average Days on Market, say more than 180 days, you need to factor this into your numbers. It may still be a good deal, but you need to factor in the extra carrying cost if you are planning to put a property back on the market after a rehab. Also, until you have more experience with bridge loans or rehab loans, I would recommend staying in familiar neighborhoods in a price range that is roughly plus or minus 30 percent of the median home value for that area.

The Local Venue. You or someone on your team need to have a thorough understanding of the laws, unique rules, taxes, codes, zoning requirements, and court cases that could have an impact on your investment in a particular neighborhood. This part is so important that I generally have an attorney do the investigation and research for me. Unless you understand all the legal factors you're facing in a local venue, you could step into some difficulties you had not anticipated. For example, one time we were considering making a hard money bridge loan on a property in California. Our due diligence was nearly complete when our attorney came across a couple of court cases from the local judge. In these court cases, the judge had ruled contrary to the state law regarding usury. In fact, he had a history of effectively declaring certain normal business loans as usurious, even though they were below the state's statutory interest rate levels. This was of particular concern to us since we make high interest rates on bridge loans.

Why do a deal in a jurisdiction where the local court purposely counteracts the state law? Sure, the issue might never arise if the property does well, but if the loan goes into default, you may very well get challenged legally on potential usury. Suddenly you'll find yourself in court spending time and energy that you could have been using to do a dozen other hard money deals in jurisdictions where usury is not an issue. The same can be said for water issues, past due utility debts, etc. That's why it's important to have a local attorney help you with your due diligence, especially when in an unfamiliar venue.

Terms. Obviously the terms of the agreement are important whether you're making an equity investment or a loan. If it's an equity investment, what percentage of the ownership would you have? What is the upside? Are there tax benefits to ownership? You should never let the tax tail wag the investment dog, but if a deal is borderline, a favorable tax situation might be the deciding factor in determining that the deal is worth doing. If it is a loan, what is the interest rate, the origination points, and the time frame? Your attorney will probably also suggest a default interest rate and maybe even default points to be paid, or loan extension fees.

> *"Successful people don't avoid risks. They learn to manage them. They don't dive off cliffs into unexplored waters. They learn how deep the water is, and make sure there are no hidden obstacles. Then they plunge in."*
>
> ~ Nido Qubein

You also need to factor in whether it is a personal loan or a business loan. Usury laws can vary in some jurisdictions based on the type of loan. There is an infinite variety of terms that can be put together. I would suggest that you start with a structure that your attorney is familiar with and is acceptable in your area, then adjust from there to make the deal profitable, low risk, and feasible in the local market. Don't forget to have your attorney weigh in on your adjustments. I prefer bridge loans with an interest rate of 15 percent or higher, with 4 to 8 origination points and loan-to-value ratios under 65 percent. If I see that there can be a lot of upside in a property, I might add a convertible feature to the loan so that I have the option of converting the loan over to an equity position or to include an equity share agreement.

On equity deals, I prefer to enter way down the sale chain at a wholesale price. This helps lower the risk and provides a higher probability for a successful exit.

Business Model. You need to take a very close look at the business model of the deal, paying particular attention to several key factors, including:

- **How will it make money?** You should be able to simplify all the details down to precisely how a business or real estate project will make money. Evaluate everything against this. Pay attention to the details and have situational awareness.

- **What is the source of the income?** Will you be earning interest and origination points on a loan? Or will you reap your profit from an equity gain after the property is rehabilitated and sold? Or will you generate your profits from increased cash flow from higher rental income on a multi-family investment? Is there also a good possibility of earning capital gains in a few years? If the project is a business turn-around, where and how will the business earn its income?

- **How do investors get paid?** What is the pecking order of payment? Does the deal stipulate that investors are the first ones to be paid or last ones?

- **What could go wrong?** Spend some time brainstorming and coming up with a list of things that could go wrong on the deal. What is the worst case scenario? The best case scenario? The expected or most likely case scenario? Is the project routine? Have similar projects been done by this team many times before or is there something unique about this project that the team will be encountering for the first time on this project?

Plan B, Plan C, Plan D – Have more than one exit plan before you enter.

- **What if the initial exit plan goes wrong?** What is the back-up plan? When you watch a James Bond movie, you'll see that something always goes wrong when he's trying to save the world. But what does he do? Does he quit and say "ah shucks, it didn't work out according to plan and now the world will come to an end?" No, he comes up with a Plan B, sometimes even a Plan C or a Plan D. He improvises. He innovates. He persists. He and his team do whatever needs to be done to achieve the objective.

- **If the borrower defaults on your bridge loan, what is your Plan B? Plan C?** If you structure the deal correctly and only close deals that have a low loan-to-value ratio, you will likely make more money by foreclosing on the loan and then selling the property yourself, than you did on the loan. Maybe Plan C is to foreclose on the loan, get control of the property and then lease it. The important point is that these things need to be thoroughly

> *"Remember that the cards you're dealt are less important than the way you play your hand."*
>
> ~ Nido Qubein

planned up front during the homework stage—before you close on the initial investment. If you are looking at a deal that has no Plan B or Plan C, where *everything* has to go right to make money, maybe you should walk away from the deal and move on to a better deal elsewhere.

100-Day Launch Plan

The concept of developing a 100-day launch plan is relatively new, but I think it is important. It's something that should be carefully laid out before the deal is closed. Some might say that technically a 100-Day Launch Plan is not part of due diligence. For me it is.

The reason is that you can roughly test the viability of a project under "what-if" scenarios. Roadblocks to success on a project may be revealed and better to know about those while you still have time to change your mind and walk away from the deal. For one thing, you need to determine how the cash from the investment is going to be used. That information is often outlined in a "Uses of Funds" statement, or a "Uses of Cash" statement. It is also very important to have a timeline attached to the Uses of Funds statement.

For example, over the next 100 days, how much of the rehab work of a project will be done? When will the property go on the market? It would take just a little common sense to see whether the 100-Day launch plan is reasonable or overly optimistic. The 100-Day launch plan can also be used to see if the deal terms are correctly matched to the project. For instance, it would clearly be a mistake to offer a six-month bridge loan on a rehab or building project that will take nine months to complete.

There is much wisdom in the old saying, "Take the original schedule, estimate and double it; that schedule will be closer to reality." Overly optimistic schedules lead to cost overruns. They reduce profits and increase risk.

Those are the types of issues that you should be able to uncover in a 100-Day Plan. Also with a good 100-Day launch plan you may be able to finds ways to accelerate progress on the project. Achieving your goals more quickly can both reduce risk and increase the rate of return. Speed of implementation can be improved by careful review of the 100-Day Launch Plan....and keep you lined up *Right to the Money.*

"Our survey found that in 60 percent of cases, businesses [included as part of a Private Equity portfolio] had 100-day plans or similar which mapped out the actions to be taken by management, together with timescales. While the majority of private equity firms made significant contributions to developing the plan, only about one-third were said to be actively involved in its implementation."

~ Working with Private Equity Portfolio Companies,
January 2013 KPMG

"Ninety percent of politicians give the other 10 percent a bad reputation. "

- Henry Kissinger

Chapter 5

Build a Legacy of True Wealth

My favorite things in life don't cost any money. It is really clear that the most precious resource we all have is time.

-- Steve Jobs

What is true wealth? It's everything we have that money can't buy and death can't take away. As we be build our lives, relationships, and business, we lay the foundation for our legacy, and true wealth is really all that matters. I'm constantly reminded of this because it is one of our core values—something we aspire to deliver to all the people in our lives every day and to everyone we are able to touch.

My friend, the late George Ernest Busse, exemplified that concept in everything he did. His mantra in life was: *"You haven't lived until you do something nice for someone who may never expect it and can never repay it."*

Throughout his life, George accumulated true wealth—not in material things, but in the lives he touched. He was one of the most selfless, most generous individuals in his community.

True wealth comes in many forms. If you live life to the fullest, give back to your community and to those around you, maintain a fiscally-responsible, self-reliant lifestyle, and build a legacy for future generations, you will have achieved true wealth. Let's look at some of the key ingredients of true wealth:

Money

You may not need a lot of money to make your impact on the world, but it could certainly help. Managing your money effectively and accumulating wealth can be vital to a fulfilling life. It's important to earn a reasonable rate of return on your investments and minimize your risks, as we have outlined earlier.

> *"No one would remember the Good Samaritan if he'd only had good intentions--he had money as well."*
>
> - Margaret Thatcher

But sometimes the things you invest in can be even more important than your rate of return. For instance, tobacco stocks pay a great dividend and have a long history of outstanding growth, but do you really want to invest in products that cause severe health problems and lead to hundreds of thousands of deaths each year? There are many superb, positive companies you can invest in. Try to put your money in the companies that have a good return ANS that can make the world a better place—whether that's food, technology, medicine, or important services. You can do this and earn a good rate of return while minimizing risk. It's a matter of choice.

I am not saying go out and find green businesses to invest in, or to find companies whose only redeeming quality is that they qualify for special tax incentive credits from Uncle Sam. I generally don't like investments where the main benefit is the tax credit. The tax credit distorts ordinary economic logic and skews judgments. This often leads to the tax tail wagging the investment dog.

While I am fine with green investments, I am generally distrustful of companies that have an aggressive PR campaign to only show the world that they are green, sometimes trying to show that they are greener then they really are. Why so much emphasis on telling the world about their green projects? Sometimes, like a magician, some companies focus your attention in one area to distract attention from their less savory activities elsewhere. You can maximize your contribution to the world and your legacy by choosing companies, causes, and ventures that are both profitable and make the world a better place.

Health

As Mahatma Gandhi once said, *"It is health that is real wealth and not pieces of gold and silver."* Without your health, you really have nothing. You can't make a living, you can't enjoy life, you can't fully enjoy your important relationships, and you can't make a contribution to society without good health. Your health is what gives you the ability to live life to the fullest and the drive and energy to earn a good living and make an impact on the world around you.

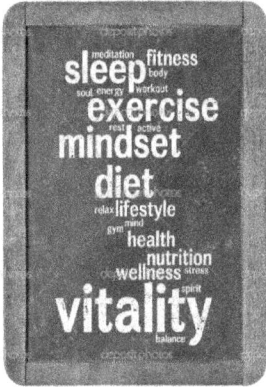

You have an obligation to yourself, to your family and friends and to the world at large to do all you can to maintain your health, vitality, and your strength. That means avoiding bad habits and excessive behavior, exercising regularly and eating a healthy diet. It means monitoring your health with regular visits to the doctor, and taking the time and effort to keep your body functioning on all cylinders for as long as possible.

Only with good health can you achieve the things that are important to your life and to contribute to the wellbeing of those around you and to the world at large. Above all else, do everything in your power to stay in good health through a healthy lifestyle, regular exercise and a nutritious diet, because without your health, everything else in your life will suffer.

Relationships

Good friends, a loving relationship with your spouse or partner, and an engaged, ongoing interaction with your children, your parents and your other close relatives can help you live a happy and rewarding life while adding to the enjoyment and fulfillment of your loved ones.

While there are always temptations to stray from your committed relationships, you can simplify your life and bring more energy to the positive things that are important to you by maintaining loyal relationships with those who are closest to you. If you have children, you have an obligation to give those children all the time, energy and resources you can muster to provide them with the best possible chance of a successful career and a happy existence. There is no better, more fulfilling, more appropriate and important responsibility in life than to prepare your children for a well-balanced, successful life.

That may mean helping them with their homework, coaching their soccer team, attending their concerts and awards programs, taking them on trips and adventures. It may mean spending less time golfing with your buddies or joining your colleagues for a drink after work, but there is no better use of your time than spending it with your kids.

Powerful Life Experiences

Life is a privilege, a rare opportunity to walk this earth and enjoy the benefits of living in the greatest, most prosperous nation in the history of the world. Despite all the fiscal and debt problems that are at every level of government, most of the poorest people today live better lives than the richest kings and queens of a few hundred years ago. It is an opportunity that should be cherished and exploited. Don't waste it. See the world. Try new things. Challenge yourself to try experiences that you've never had a chance to do before, to learn new skills and embark on adventures to see new places, meet new people and engage in activities you've never done before. It's important to keep life fresh and to eschew the same old routine. To live life to the fullest, you need to step outside your comfort zone. The only way to grow as a person is to continue to be open to new experiences, adventures and opportunities. One of the best

> *When you are through learning, you are through.*
> - Will Rogers

> *"Some people wonder all their lives if they've made a difference. The Marines don't have that problem."*
> - Ronald Reagan

> *"When you're finished changing, you're finished."*
> - Benjamin Franklin

> *"Accumulate good memories."*
> - Nido Qubein

things about growing older is that there can be more of a sense of drinking in life's moments, rather than letting them whiz by.

Make sure that some of your life experiences come in the form of helping others. Spend some time volunteering at a food bank or a homeless shelter, join a trip with Habitat for Humanity and travel to a storm-ravaged area to help rebuild a community. Volunteer to teach underprivileged children or coach a sports team. Everything you give to others—time, energy, money and other resources—helps build your true legacy here on earth and gives you the satisfaction of making a difference in the lives of others.

But most of all don't waste the opportunity to live your life to the fullest, to see the world and to experience the excitement of life in its many forms. You only go around once in life. Make sure you get the most from your time here.

> *"Life is not a journey to the grave with the intention of arriving safely in a well-preserved body, but, rather, to skid in broadside in a cloud of smoke, at the very last moment, thoroughly used up, totally worn out, and loudly proclaiming, 'Wow ! What a ride!"*
>
> — Mark Frost

Building Your Legacy

What does this mean exactly? We tend to think of a legacy as the money and possessions we leave behind for our family and loved ones. But your legacy can go well beyond your will or your money. And it can mean different things for different people. If you're wealthy, it may mean contributing to your place of worship to fund charitable efforts or help finance a new wing. It may mean contributing to your community by donating to campaigns to build a community center, a sports field for youth or a museum or arts center others can enjoy. It may mean starting your own non-profit business to

help others or donating to foreign missions to help people in need around the world.

But you don't necessarily need a lot of money to build your legacy. Donating your time and energy to help out at your church or community center, to help others in need by volunteering your time for an organization or fund-raising campaign, or putting your skills to work to renovate homes for the poor or help children improve their skills or succeed in school can all contribute to your legacy. I have seen thousands of people in retirement. My observation is that the most happy and fulfilled ones are those that are giving of their time to help, teach, or mentor others.

The goal in building your legacy is to give more than you take during your time on earth. And like most of the good deeds we do in life, the power of giving time can not only help the lives of others but can bring purpose and meaning to your life as well.

> *"You can't connect the dots looking forward; you can only connect them looking backward. So you have to trust that the dots will somehow connect in your future, you have to trust in something – your gut, destiny, life, karma, whatever. This approach has never let me down, and it has made all the difference in my life."*
>
> ■ Steve Jobs

Your 'To-Do', 'Stop-Doing' and 'To-Be' Lists

We've all heard of a "to-do" list. Writing down all the things you want to accomplish for the day or over a given period of time can help you focus on the things that are most important to you. The busier you get the more important it is to jot down a regular to-do list. As more details clog your brain, your memory becomes weaker. You lose track of the tasks that are most important. A to-do list can help organize your life and keep you on-track to do the things that are most important to your success.

But there are a couple of other lists you might also want to add to your life:

A 'Stop Doing' List

There may be a number of bad habits you've fallen into that you would like to rid from your life. The best way to end the habits that degrade your life or your career and detract from your focus is to identify those habits and write them down on a "stop-doing" list. It can be unhealthy habits like smoking, drinking too much, or eating unhealthy foods, or less obvious bad habits, such as procrastinating too much, wasting too much time surfing the computer or watching TV, making excuses when things don't go your way, or failing to focus on your important goals.

We have all heard the expression "garbage in, garbage out." For many of us, a more accurate description might be "garbage in, garbage stays, then garbage gets pregnant and multiplies itself." At some point, we need to stop collecting garbage and start ridding ourselves of it. We all have habits in life we'd like to break. The first step in the process is to identify them and write them down.

There may also be some things that you continually put on your to-do list that never seem to get done. This could be an indication that it is not of enough priority to your life. Maybe then you should put this task on you stop doing list. Get rid of clutter. Favor simplicity.

A 'To-Be' List

Even before you write your to-do list each day, you might want to start writing a "to-be" list. What do you want from your life? What is important to you? What are the things you might overlook in your everyday routine? For instance, would you like to be more open-minded, kinder and more considerate, more appreciative of each day, more generous and charitable, happier, more focused, more affluent, more frugal, or more ambitious? Write it all down on your list. By identifying the qualities that you would like to bring to your life—and writing them down regularly—you can give yourself a better chance of reaching those goals and living a more fulfilling life, the kind of life you've always hoped to live. Writing them done is the first step to turning these to-be visions into a reality.

The Table on the next offers many examples of the things you might want to include in your "to-be list:"

Table 3. *To-Be List*

Stick to your core values	We all grow up with some core values that are important in our approach to life. Never lose sight of those core values and make them an ongoing aspect of your life.
Be driven by your life purpose	What's your purpose in life? What do you see as your life legacy? Stay on task and maintain your drive to achieve those things that you consider most important. It helps to have a purpose in life that drives you to do great things.
Be frugal but not stingy	It's okay to be fiscally conservative, even frugal. No need to spend lavishly, but don't be so tight with your money that you deny yourself and others the opportunity to get the most out of life. Be less concerned about how much things cost you and more concerned about how much value, health, happiness, or fulfillment they bring to your children, your family, your world, and yourself.
Cherish your relationships	You're very fortunate if you have great friends, a family, parents, brothers, sisters, a loving spouse, and loving children. It's a lonely life without friends and family. Always cherish those relationships and put in the effort you need to maintain them.
Value your health	Without your health, your quality of life takes a serious hit. Do everything you can to stay fit and healthy. Doctors can help, but ultimately you are the one responsible for your health by the activities you pursue, the diet you consume, and the bad habits you avoid.
Wisely manage your financial resources	By working, saving and investing wisely throughout your life you can prepare for a prosperous retirement. Don't get greedy and take ill-advised risks. Manage your money carefully—it can be vital to your life and your legacy.
Find ways to be compassionate	Be compassionate and charitable whenever you get the chance. Never pass up an opportunity to help someone or show someone you care.
Be open to wise counselors	Avoid tunnel vision in your life by being open to the observations and advice of your family, friends and colleagues. That doesn't mean you have to follow every bit of advice that comes your way, but we can all change for the better if we're open to the suggestions of others.

Chapter 6

Respect Capital

To have a Right to the Money, *Respecting Capital* is a must-have attitude. It is an attitude that drives important decisions, actions, and priorities. Attitude determines how you set your priorities. The way you handle fire, determines if it improves your life or destroys it. Fire, properly used in a furnace, can heat your home; fire used the wrong way can burn your house down. Similarly, *Respecting Capital* can attract a great deal more money into your life style. Not *Respecting Capital* will cause money to flee from your hands.

While I worked for a management consulting firm in Washington D.C. in the 80's, I was very fortunate to meet Sean McCarthy, a retired Marine Corp veteran who had built a substantial real estate portfolio from literally nothing. Sean told me how money always flows to where it is treated the best. Most people know, or have heard of the statistic, that more than 90 percent of all the money in the world is controlled by less than 10 percent of the people. You can make the case that the specific numbers or percentages are a bit higher or lower, but the point is most of the wealth in the world is controlled by a small number of people. As a theoretical exercise, what would happen if all of the money in the world was taken from everyone and then evenly re-distributed, so that everyone started out with the same amount of money? How would money flow? Who would acquire more wealth? Who would lose wealth?

More importantly, what traits would attract money? What traits would repel money? I have talked to hundreds of people about this that has been very successful financially. Although my informal surveys may not have been specifically or statistically proper, the general consensus was that within one generation, most of the wealth would again be concentrated back in the hands of the 10 percent.

This is true for individuals, for families, for small businesses, and for large corporations. Over time, it is even true for governments large and small. The point is that money flows to where it is treated best, to where capital is respected. Capital that is put at extreme foolish risk will leave those hands. Capital that is subject to exorbitant taxes will flee that jurisdiction.

Successful investors *Respect Capital*. I don't mean to imply *Respecting Capital* as if to honor money at the altar as the most sacred thing in the world. I do suggest *Respecting Capital*, just as one should respect their ancestors, family members, and the Flag. *Respecting Capital* means having a degree of deference for money that is put to work in a commendable manner providing valuable goods and services. It means holding positive esteem for capital and recognizing its certain privileges, powers, and of course, the enormous responsibility that comes with it.

The unsophisticated investor often does not respect capital. Many small investors do not respect capital, and as a result, they never become a large investor. In fact, some people envy people who have accumulated a lot of capital. Envious people, like critics, are often broke. For some, it is easier to find fault with something that they cannot attain rather than go through the hard work to attain it. Those who do respect capital are more likely to become successful investors. The little guy has little experience, little capital, and little wisdom. They see little difference between investing and gambling. Respecting Capital is about <u>not</u> wasting money.

It is also about <u>not</u> recklessly exposing money to unnecessary or extreme risk. It is about squeezing as much of the risk out of a deal as possible. I like to invest in companies or real estate projects where the management and leadership team *Respects Capital*. Where they act and make decisions like "owners" rather than employees. Where expenses and budgets are monitored, controlled, and adhered to.

During the recent real estate bubble–powered by thousands of zombie loans– one of the most destructive issues was the lack of respect for capital at many levels:

by buyers, lenders, appraisers, the Wall Street firms that sold the mortgage backed securities, and others.

There are many things people can do to *Respect Capital*:

1. Focus on higher return, lower risk opportunities.

Don't risk a lot to make a little. According to conventional wisdom, the higher the rate of return on an investment, the higher the risk of that investment.

And certainly there are investments that can be demonstrated that offer a higher return with proportionately higher risk.   But people assume that all investments fit the high return, higher risk profile or low return, low risk profile.

Risk and Reward

C

A   B

Low Risk   Medium Risk   High Risk   Very High Risk

All investments do not nicely fit onto line indicated in the Risk and Reward Figure. Not true if you choose to take the Red Pill and see the world as it really is. There are investments that have low return expectations *AND* are also high risk. See the lower right quadrant area, labeled B, of the Risk and Reward Figure. These are investments that could be at best characterized as "foolish".   There are also investments that have high return potential and low risk.   See the upper left quadrant, labeled C, of the Risk and Reward Figure.

It is obviously better to diversify into a number of these investments that have the better return—lower risk profiles. First chart line, high return must take higher risk—that's conventional thinking. But that does not mean all investments fit on that line. Some investments in fact are high risk and low return. You want to find those that are high return and low risk.

Sure, it takes some work to uncover these. Or align with a partner or with people in your network who have the ability to find and manage low risk, higher return opportunities.

> *"I just wait until there is money lying in the corner, and all I have to do is go over there and pick it up. I do nothing in the meantime."*
> ■ Jim Rogers, Market Wizards

2. Live Below Your Means.

> *It is impossible to get wealthy if you spend more money than you make.*
> ■ J. Paul Getty
> *"Beware of little expenses. A small leak will sink a great ship."*
> ■ Benjamin Franklin

At first glance, the power of this wisdom—to spend less than you make—seems obvious. In his book, *The Millionaire Next Door* author Thomas J. Stanley offers many examples to make this point very clear. Most mega-millionaires become wealthy not by making a ton of money, but by saving, investing, and compounding modest amounts over time, and by living below their means. Spend less than you earn, invest your savings wisely, and you can grow wealthy.

Technically, this is all true. However, in my opinion, *the real power of living below your means is that it changes your attitude, and over time, gives you super-human decision-making powers about money.* It can dramatically increase your probability of success. It is *Respecting Capital.*

But living below your means can be difficult no matter how much money you have. Lottery winners and ex-sports stars have been notorious for blowing their entire fortunes with nothing to show for it. No matter how much you make, you need to adopt a savings mentality—in which saving money becomes a priority in your life that outweighs all of the finer trappings of life that tempt you to open your wallet. Oil tycoon T. Boone Pickens, despite his billions of dollars of assets, has never lost his appreciation of frugality. In a 2012 interview he told *Kiplinger's* magazine: "People are always surprised that I don't have a closetful of suits. I buy three suits every five years or so and only own ten, total. That's all I need."

If you want to become wealthy, do as the wealthy do, and *Respect Your Capital*. *Respect Your Capital*, whether it is a small amount or a large family fortune. Respect other's Capital.

Richard Russell explains this powerful attitude in his highly acclaimed writings at DowTheoryLetters.com:

*"In the investment world, the wealthy investor has one major advantage over the little guy, the stock market amateur and the neophyte trader. The advantage that the wealthy investor enjoys is that **he doesn't need the markets.** I can't begin to tell you what a difference that makes, both in one's mental attitude and in the way one actually handles one's money.*

The wealthy investor doesn't need the markets, because he already has all the income he needs. He has money coming in via bonds, T-bills, money market funds, stocks, alternative investments, and real estate. In other words, the wealthy investor never feels pressured to "make money" in the market.

The wealthy investor tends to be an expert on values. When bonds are cheap and bond yields are irresistibly high, he buys bonds. When stocks are on the bargain table and stock yields are attractive, he buys stocks. When select sectors of real estate are a great value, he buys real estate. When great art or fine jewelry or gold is on the "give away" table, he buys art or diamonds or gold. In other words, the wealthy investor puts his money where the great values are.

And if no outstanding values are available, the wealthy investor waits. He can afford to wait. He has money coming in daily, weekly, monthly. The wealthy investor knows what he is looking for, and he doesn't mind waiting months, or even years, for his next investment. (They call that patience).

But what about the little guy? The one who lives above his means? This fellow always feels pressured to "make money." And, in return, he's always pressuring the market to "do something" for him. But sadly, the market isn't interested. When the little guy isn't buying stocks offering 1 percent or 2 percent yields, he's off to Las Vegas or Atlantic City trying to beat the house at roulette. Or he's spending 20 bucks a week on lottery tickets, or he's "investing" in some crackpot scheme that his neighbor told him about (in strictest confidence, of course).

And because the little guy is trying to force the market to do something for him, he's a guaranteed loser. The little guy doesn't understand values so he constantly overpays. He doesn't comprehend the power of compounding, and he doesn't understand money. He's never heard the adage, "He who understands interest–earns it. He who doesn't understand interest–pays it." The little guy is the typical American, and he's deeply in debt. **And he does not live below his means. He spends more than he makes.**

The little guy is in hock up to his ears. As a result, he's always sweating–sweating to make payments on his house, his refrigerator, his car or his lawn mower. He's impatient, and he feels perpetually put upon. He tells himself that he has to make money—and fast. And he dreams of those "big, juicy mega-bucks." In the end, the little guy wastes his money in the market, or he loses his money gambling, or he dribbles it away on senseless schemes. In short, this "money-nerd" spends his life trying to dash up the financial down-escalator. Why run against the wind? Put the wind at your back. But here's the ironic part of it. If, from the beginning, the little guy had adopted a strict policy of never spending more than he made, if he had taken his extra savings and compounded it in intelligent, income-producing investments, then in due time he'd have money coming in daily, weekly, monthly, just like the rich man. The little guy would have become a financial winner, instead of a loser."

Living below your means does not mean that you have to spend up to your means. Save, respect, and invest the money not needed to meet your lifestyle expenses.

> If your outflow exceeds your inflow, then your upkeep will be your downfall.

Learn how to live as well as a Billionaire without a billion dollars:

www.RightToTheMoney.com/SpecialBonus3

3. Give with Gratitude

Respecting Capital does not mean being stingy with money. It means putting money where it will provide or produce good value. Sometimes this money is invested in your business, sometimes it is invested in other businesses, and sometimes it is invested in charity. Many churches, religions, and charities espouse the virtue of giving money. Some, for example, say to give 10 percent of all you earn. It would be easy to assume that cutting costs and reducing donations to charity is an easy way to save money, to *Respect Capital. But it is exactly the opposite.* Money that is given to the universe has a way of multiplying and coming back to you ten times over, all the while making the world a better place as it circulates. Energy stored in battery provides no value until the electricity circulates. Similarly, the power of money is realized as it circulates and is invested and exchanged around the economy.

When you give money, don't give it grudgingly. Give it happily, give it with a warm heart, with gratitude, with the highest level of thankfulness you have on Thanksgiving Day. Attach your blessing, and honor those dollars as you send them into the world. Money is a symbol of energy and it attaches to the energy that you impart to it. Money is not good or bad. Money is simply a tool that can magnify your impact on the world. Choose to add your positive gratitude to the money you give. You decide what energy that you impart to it. Don't be tight, be *Right to the Money.*

4. Teach your Children Well

Like many good things in life, financial success can be a double-edged sword, especially if you have kids. Most families face a tremendous dilemma: how do you raise financially responsible, prosperous, and self-reliant children? This might be even more challenging to do for wealthy families. Especially when you consider the attitudes responsible for your own success are not shared by many in the upcoming generation. Can you give them a taste of the good life that you worked so hard to achieve without spoiling them?

In my opinion, this is one of the most critical ideas that will shape our future world. You may have heard the old expression, "shirt sleeves to short sleeves in three generations." The first generation, works hard to build the family fortune, the second generation is coasting, not expanding the fortune and often dissipating the fortune, so that the third generation has to start over and work to build a new fortune.

Melanie Jane Nicolas offers a few wisdoms from excerpts in her book, *Raising Wealthy Kids:*

"Do you know what is important and often overlooked because we are so busy every day to make ends meet? Instilling in our children early on a sense of responsibility and leadership and of how wealth is really created. To teach them money management, business skills, and rugged individualism. And to make it fun as we plant seeds so they will have a head start. There's no need for them to be like other children who think they are entitled to something. These children who understand wealth will turn into adults that can really make things happen and change the world."

"The most important thing you can do, and if you apply this with your kids it'll make a huge change in their financial well-being, is to model great financial behaviors. Dr. Nido Quebin says, "We live. They watch. They learn." Watch what you say, do and experience with money. And continuous education is needed to do this. As parents, we can't expect our kids to be financially

responsible if we aren't financially responsible. It takes patience and intentional and purposeful actions that are congruent with our family's core money values.

"Whatever you demonstrate to your children on a daily basis about how you manage and spend your money gives them the opportunity either to choose to do what you do, or not. The period of development from birth to eight years old is referred to as the 'imprint period." It is the period of their life that children copy what people do in the world around them without conscious awareness. The people they spend most of their time with are who they most likely choose to copy or model. So think about financial freedom to manifest it in your life and model it to your children.

"One of the most powerful habits I model — and the one we know wealthy people do on a regular basis—is to pay yourself first. While most people pay everyone else first on a regular basis and don't have enough money to save and invest, I teach my kids that paying yourself first is one of the first habits they need to start on the road to financial freedom. Now some kids feel they can't pay themselves first because they don't have a lot of money. Well, can they pay themselves 50 cents? It's not about the amount you can pay yourself first; it is about the act of paying yourself first that counts, because once it becomes a habit, it will be easier and easier to do. Some other wealth habits I model for my kids are using cash instead of credit cards, watching Shark Tank with my kids instead of meaningless shows, and creating wealth by running my business. Watch what you model to your kids because they are picking up on your habits. Some examples of when I talk to my kids about money are:

- *I allow them to help me write checks or pay bills online.*
- *I bring my kids along when I deposit money at the bank and involve them in the financial decisions and research when I'm talking to the banker.*
- *I take my daughter to rental properties to teach her real estate investing."*

Melanie Jane Nicolas has many more powerful ideas on *Raising Wealthy Kids.* I especially liked her section on "Ten Keys to Raising Young Entrepreneurs."

You can get her book at **www.RaisingWealthyKidsBook.com.**

> *"Children are educated by what the grown-up is, and not by their talk."*
> ■ Carl Jung

I believe it is important to instill good habits in kids. Habits that should be worked on within households that want to *Respect Capital* include:

- Pay yourself first

- Saving versus spending

- Learning and appreciating the difference between needs and wants

- Solving problems in ways other than using money. For example, my son got a flat tire on his bike. The simplest solution would have been to drop the bike off at a repair shop and have it fixed. Instead, we took the bike apart, drained the remaining air out, removed the inner tube, bought an inexpensive patch kit, repaired the tube, inflated it in water to check for leaks, reinstalled the tube and put the bike back together. More steps, but my kids learned several things with this experience, including that sometimes (even in our instant gratification, charge-the-credit-card economy) there are ways to solve problems with little or less money.

- Compounding

- Learning about the value of things

- Comparison shopping. Compare similar products with different prices and different features.

- Becoming self-reliant

- Not just relying on only books, internet, and schools for education. Get out and see the world. Kids often learn more on field trips than in classrooms.

- Learning history. Link book knowledge of history to personal travel to historical places
- Learning to think

4. Take Care of Business Details

Within minutes of entering a business you can often get a very good idea if capital is respected in that business. Simple things such as cleanliness, the way customers are greeted, how complaints are handled, even as to whether or not the plants are watered. A Chinese philosopher once made the point that good Feng Shui is not just about how certain items are arranged as part of a home's interior design or how the landscaping is designed outside of an office building. Rather, it is more important to see how these things were used and cared for.

For example, he entered a store that had a reasonably healthy supply of customers, good employees, and good, desirable products. But near the door, he noticed a house plant that was wilting. It needed water from an owner who was too busy for the details. The philosopher chose not to shop at that store because he could see that there was poor Feng Shui energy on the part of the owners. A few weeks later he returned to the store. There were fewer customers in the store, and the wilted plant was now dead. A few months after that, the store was closed and had been forced out of business.

> *"In my youth, I traveled much, and I observed in different countries, that the more public provisions were made for the poor, the less they provided for themselves, and of course became poorer. And, on the contrary, the less was done for them, the more they did for themselves, and became richer."*
>
> ■ Ben Franklin

Not taking care of simple details can ruin a business. It was not the lack of watering the plant that killed the business. It was the attitude of the owner–those details were not a priority–that killed the business. The dead plant was simply an indicator of inattention to detail. It is in the compounding of many details where great success or great failure is determined.

When customers or business buyers come into your business, they are going to judge your location, visibility, signage, and curb appeal. They are going to make a judgment on whether they think the business is busy or slow, whether the owner runs a tight ship, whether the employees are dressed professionally, whether the staff is courteous and so on. And every detail will have an effect on the willingness of the customers to spend their money at the store—and return again as repeat customers.

> *"Even a small leak can sink a great ship."*
> ~Ben Franklin

The Large Print Giveth and the Small Detailed Print Taketh Away

---

For Want of a Nail
For want of a nail the shoe was lost.
For want of a shoe the horse was lost.
For want of a horse the rider was lost.
For want of a rider the message was lost.
For want of a message the battle was lost.
For want of a battle the kingdom was lost.
And all for the want of a horseshoe nail.

~14th Century Proverb

5. Use All Forms of Capital

When I say *all forms of capital*, I'm not referring to just financial forms of capital, like stocks or bonds. I'm referring to different types of capital. Money is one form of capital. Capital also includes other resources to get things done. For example, your Rolodex (or electronic versions today) could symbolize your *Relational Capital*. Another could be human capital (labor). You can often get great insight into how a business is doing without studying its books in detail, but simply by observing how other forms of capital are put to work. I love to take a look at various businesses or real estate projects to see how other non-money forms of capital are being put to work, instead of just writing a check to solve a problem.

I had a property once that was experiencing a gradual decline in new rental applications in a market where competing properties were experiencing solid increases in rents and occupancy rates. The onsite property manager was trying to convince me to approve extra advertising expenses for a radio campaign in order to increase the occupancy rate. After further investigation, I discovered a much easier and cheaper solution.

It turned out the "For Rent" sign that was usually visible to drive-by traffic was now obscured by overgrown tree branches. Once we trimmed the tree branches to expose the sign, the rental applications returned to their normal levels. Simply throwing money at the problem can often cover up the root of the problem—and the logical solution.

Before you write a check to solve a problem, try to identify the underlying issue that created the problem in the first place. Common sense can go a long way.

Practice Respecting Capital by applying the above steps.

Succeeding in business can be very similar to succeeding in sports. If you want to excel, you have to practice. Golfers practice. Tennis players practice. Basketball players are constantly on the court shooting baskets. If they want to succeed, they know they have to practice. Practice can give you a slight edge.

In business, if you want to be in the zone and become the best you can be in the things you're doing, you have to practice. Sean McCarthy, one of my early mentors, used to say that you could even practice your negotiating skills by going into a 7-Eleven store and asking for a discount on their donuts. Yes, a donut is a small item, but practicing your skills in negotiating a discount for your donuts can help you prepare for negotiating discounts on other things later, like a real estate investment. Asking for a discount on donuts is easy, especially if the donuts are not hot-from-oven fresh. It's not the size of the discount that matters, it's the act of asking for the discount that will help you become better at *Respecting Capital*.

There are many aspects of *Respecting Capital*, and they all are important to your success. If you want to thrive in business and in life, you need to look for higher return, lower risk opportunities, live below your means, give with gratitude, teach your children well, focus on the details, use all the forms of capital that are available to you, and then practice all of those skills to become the best you can be in all phases of your life and business.

You have a *Right to the Money*, and you'll give yourself the best possible chance to cash in on that right by *Respecting Capital*.

Chapter 7

Build Relational Capital to Enhance Financial Capital

Of all the methods of *Right to the Money* we have discussed so far, the seventh is the most powerful. Building relational capital can cut years off the time it takes to reach your financial goals and to reach "escape velocity."

This one is far more valuable than getting into a good investment or saving thousands of dollars in taxes. It is also much more valuable because it can dramatically improve your wealth, your business prosperity, your health, your social life, and every other aspect of your life.

It is something I have spent my lifetime building – my *relational capital. Proper application of Relational Capital can multiply Financial Capital many times.*

Properly cultivated, *Relational Capital* can give you Super Human Powers! It can have similar impacts as *The Force*, but use it like Luke Skywalker, not Darth Vader.

Relational capital is the single most important key to success in business. There is nothing else that has been more important to both my success and the success of most self-made individuals than relationship capital and all of the opportunities it brings from key contacts, associations and friendships with other accomplished people. In fact, there are no "self-made" people. Every single "self-made" person became the person they are with the help of others; some achievers got a high degree of help from people, others got less, but everyone got there with help from others. I think a better term is "self-starter", rather than self-made.

I have had a very lucky run of great teachers in my life, and I have found myself with the opportunity to pass along some of the lessons I have learned from them to others. One of them was Sean McCarthy, about 25 years ago when I was working for a management consulting firm in Washington, D.C. Sean was a self-starter, a Vietnam veteran, an extremely successful investor, and a savvy street-smart businessman.

He invited me to invest with him in some deals involving high-yield, hard money loans to real estate and energy companies based on the value of their collateral, reserves and equipment. Sometimes the deals included options and equity conversions or warrants. The returns on Sean's deals were consistently in the double-digits annually, with occasional triple digit returns.

I learned real world financial and relationship strategies from Sean that were never even discussed in my MBA classes. Over the next several years, I partnered with Sean on a number of bridge financing deals, always structuring solid real estate as collateral. Sometimes we were paid back our interest and principal on the loan we made as scheduled; other times we had to foreclose on the property that was put up as collateral.

I soon learned that we made our largest profits on the deals where we were forced to take back the property via foreclosure or where we negotiated with the borrower to deed the property to us *"in lieu of foreclosure."* Sean McCarthy was one of my early, powerful connections who contributed enormously to my success.

Five Thousand Dollars an Hour

The more good contacts you make, the more opportunities that will come your way. A few years ago, an attorney I work with introduced me to an investor who taught me how she makes upwards of $5,000 per hour. Hard to believe, but true. In this instance, there was a need for a money partner—a sponsor, if you will—to help finance the purchase of an attractive apartment complex that had very good cash flow. By being a "sponsor" on the apartment acquisition, her responsibility was to "lend" her financial statements to the investor and sign as a co-borrower on a multi-million dollar FNMA loan. This involved some time for due diligence work and review to make sure it was a good deal with sound collateral.

For her time and effort she put into the project, she received a cash payment of $100,000 at the closing and an additional $180,000 three years later when she exited the deal.

Best of all, this FNMA loan was a "non-recourse" loan, meaning that, as a borrower, she had no personal liability. The apartment rents paid the mortgage, not her. If the property suffered a turn for the worse and could not make the loan payments, she was not required to put up her cash to cover the loan because it was a non-recourse loan. My point is, relational capital – connections–matter; access to the right people, ideas and deal flow can be extremely powerful.

This idea was powerful even in my early days–30 years ago–when I first purchased rental real estate. On one of my rentals, I had a tenant who skipped town without paying the rent. An associate of mine introduced me to an attorney who claimed he had connections with an FBI-trained skip tracer who could help us track down the skipped tenant in order to get paid. (Later, I discovered the attorney not only had connections with former FBI agents, but he also had other very unique and useful deal strategies.)

In hindsight, the missed rent was a small price to pay for the opportunity to line up some valuable new connections. It gave me options beyond just eating the lost rent, which enhanced my expertise and experience, and dramatically increased my confidence in doing more deals.

That's the power of relationship capital. And as my network expanded and my relational capital grew, my ability to do larger deals—and more deals—grew as well. I've since learned that relationships are not simply linear, but are better described as geometrical, even exponential. Once you connect with one person, that person can lead you to an entire network of others, some of whom will lead you still further to other contacts who can all contribute in some way to the success and growth of your business.

Anyone Can Build a Network

The good thing about networking is that anyone can do it. The example I just offered was not random luck—it was simply part of doing business. Anyone can do it. You just need to get busy, get out there and make connections. Donald Trump says that he makes more money on the golf course than Tiger Woods. Trump uses his relational capital to make, build and extend relationships on the golf course that lead to lucrative deals in his business.

If you're a neophyte in business, you might wonder why someone who is already experienced and successful would have any interest in establishing a relationship with you.

There could be many reasons. Maybe they like you. Maybe they like your energy or your eagerness to learn. Maybe you have special skills, education or expertise that they find useful. But everyone who is experienced in business understands the value of relationship capital, and they are often eager to add new blood to their network.

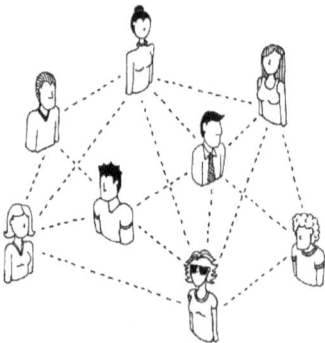

I have seen it happen hundreds of times. In some cases, I have played a very small part in introducing individuals to each other who went on to build very beneficial relationships for their businesses.

Relationship building can come in many forms—an investor in large apartment complexes introduced to an attorney to help him provide loans on apartment buildings; a world renowned industrial minerals chemist introduced to a CEO of a mining company; a start-up entrepreneur with a small budget introduced to a patent attorney who would take payment for his patent work in the form of equity in the entrepreneur's company. I've also been introduced myself to a contact who I partnered with to bid on assets at FDIC auctions when the FDIC was taking over failing banks.

I didn't match-make these deals, nor would I suggest charging a finder's fee. With the benefit of hindsight, each of these individuals would have gladly paid a finder's fee for the value that was brought to their business, but I have found benefits much greater from later introductions to other key people as "what comes around, goes around."

Relationship building is one of the most powerful perks of my job. I have the opportunity to meet other like-minded people, many of whom are successful, powerful and wealthy. While I never reveal the names of partners or key contacts, there are certainly names in my personal networks that you would recognize.

Wherever I've met my connections in my network—across the United States and around the world—I've noticed that we all have some qualities in common— self-starter, well-educated (often self-educated), affable, self-reliant, responsible and independent. My network includes real estate attorneys, specialty attorneys, insurance professionals, energy and mining experts, partners, bankers, brokers, developers, and many others. I've learned something from each of these relationships that contributes to the success of my business. The experience has shown me first hand that it's not just what you know or who you know, but many times, it's who knows you.

The fact is, no one can be an expert in every area needed to succeed in business. You need a network of experts who can help you in their special areas of expertise.

> *"Success doesn't come to you; you must go to it. The trail is well-travelled and well-marked. If you want to walk it, you can."*
> ~ Nido Qubein

Three tips to building relational capital:

1. **Be the first person in the relationship to provide value to others.** Anytime you can help someone else in your network by providing your expertise, specialized information or a referral to other contacts in your network, by all means provide that assistance to them. Most people will feel an obligation to help you later in any way that can show their appreciation for your help and to build further on your relationship.

2. **Recognize the "five and five" rule.** In five years you will have evolved habits and a life style that are most similar to the five people you spend the most time with now. So if you want to be highly successful in your business, identify five contacts who are already successful and motivated to further their success and try to spend as much time as you can with them over the next few months and years. Over time, you will be able to emulate their success. Behaviors, habits, and actions can be contagious.

3. **Take the necessary steps to infiltrate a network.** Becoming associated with a prominent network of contacts can be an important step you can take to become successful in business. But gaining trust and access to a network generally means making a significant investment of some kind—either time or money or both. That's why, like all investments, you should be judicious—bold but judicious. You need to choose your target network carefully. Find a network of people who share your interests, who have the resources to help you grow your business, and are the type of individuals you respect and enjoy.

It is important to build your relationships before you need them. You should try to be the first one to add value to the relationship. You set the pace.

If you find it difficult to identify a network that you're interested in, you might find it easier to start with an individual. In many cases, that individual might be a "node" in a network—a center of influence. The individual can help you penetrate that network through other connections.

But before you can become a successful networker, it's important to identify any of your strengths that you can bring to the table. The more value you can offer, the more accepting individuals in the network will be to your inclusion in the group.

If you don't already have an "in" to a network you'd like to join, you need to probe the network to find which *node* has an open door. Once you've found an opening, you should take whatever actions are necessary to go through that door—and that may take some type of investment on your part.

Breaking into a network effectively can't be done with a few emails or post cards. Your physical presence is required. You cannot make an impression or demonstrate a serious interest in a group unless you show up and make your presence known. Go where the network goes—whether that's a monthly meeting, a private club, an annual conference, or a periodic get-together at a local pub. Wherever members of that network assemble, you need to make an effort to be there.

One good entrée into a network can be through certain attorneys. Generally, I'm not a big fan of this profession, but attorneys can serve a useful purpose. Highly influential attorneys are often nodes in a network, whether in a particular industry or a specific location where you hope to do business.

When I travel to places in the US that are new for my business, I often make the connections I need to make by working through an attorney at that location. I systematically screen attorneys in the area until I narrow the field to about three strong candidates. I try to meet each of the candidates and make arrangements to hire the attorney I feel would be the best source for connecting me with the right people in that area who I need to meet to accommodate my business deals. It can be important to open certain doors for bigger things ahead.

No matter where you're doing business, enlisting the services of a well-connected attorney can be one of the quickest and most effective ways to penetrate a network of influential players in your industry or a new geographic market place. But whether it's through an attorney, an individual who may be a node in the network, or simply through persistent pursuit of the group you're interested in joining, aligning yourself with a prominent network can be one of the most important steps you'll ever take in getting *Right to the Money*. Once you are aligned, work to become a valuable node to others in the network.

You can read about more details on effective networking strategies in our special report, "Network Infiltration: The Secrets to Becoming a Welcome Member of the Most Exclusive Networks in the World."

www.RightToTheMoney.com/SpecialBonus4

Bonus Material

Your Inner Game

"Let me tell you about the very rich," said a character in F. Scott Fitzgerald's short story, "The Rich Boy," "They are different from you and me. They possess and enjoy wealth early, and it does something to them, makes them soft, where we are hard, cynical; where we are trustful, in a way that, unless you were born rich, it is very difficult to understand."

Times have changed since that story was penned in 1926. You don't have to be born rich, and the process of acquiring wealth does not have to be difficult to understand.

A little more than a decade after "The Rich Boy" was released, Napoleon Hill took up Andrew Carnegie's challenge to understand the rich. He interviewed hundreds of wealthy people to discern their common characteristics, and his book, *Think and Grow Rich* has sold 70 million copies since its release in 1937.

The primary principle that Hill uncovered and that I have leaned on and updated a bit (much has changed in our world in the past 75 years!) is that a person's "Inner Game" will often determine his or her destiny. **The primary difference between those who build wealth and those who beg for money on the street is not what household they were born into, it is how they think. It is the attitude that you approach the world with.**

Your level of confidence, your beliefs about yourself and the world, combined with your attitude about life comprise what some call your "Inner Game." And, like the many sports books that have been written suggesting that one's mental approach is key to victory, I would echo that idea and boldly state that your *Inner Game* will drive your destiny.

World-class athletes prove the importance of *Inner Game* all of the time. Most of them spend many hours each day working out and practicing their sport, but only a few reach the top—those who have a vastly superior *Inner Game*. In my conversations with Steven Bradbury, Olympic Gold Medal winner in short track speed skating, it was clear to me that he had an absolutely superior *Inner Game*. I saw the same sterling *Inner Game* when I met Michael Irvin, the three-time Super Bowl winner, who initially developed and then expanded his *Inner Game* from a childhood spent in poverty as one of 17 children to the massive success that he enjoys today.

Someone wisely said long ago that thoughts lead to attitudes and attitudes lead to actions. Then, actions lead to results, which determine a destiny. It all, in fact, begins in your thought life. Your *Inner Game*.

How you view the world, money, the people around you, the attitude of the universe towards you—all of these shape your attitudes and you then project those attitudes onto everyone in your world. People can instinctively sense your attitude through all stages of the day, from the vibe you give off in line at Starbucks, to the way you greet your secretary, from your first phone conversations at work to your interaction with the doorman upon returning home from the office. You are constantly giving off an attitude that reveals who you truly are.

And, if you are not careful, you can absorb the attitude of other people, for better or for worse. It is impossible to enter a stinky pig barn and then not smell stinky when you leave the barn. Don't hang around people with stinky attitudes. Hang around a rose garden to absorb the smell of roses; hang around people with a rosier attitude.

Those attitudes help to drive your actions, which will ultimately steer you to your final destination. It all begins with your *Inner Game* and it ends with your Outer Game, as you take a look and wonder how you got to where you are.

Think of this Inner Game/Outer Game relationship like a tree. What you pour in is unseen (Inner Game); it builds roots that can absorb nutrients from the ground. Your attitude will be to soak up all that is good around you as you process helpful knowledge from a variety of sources.

A tree with a healthy root system then bears beautiful branches, green leaves and delicious fruit. That is what is seen about the tree (Outer Game). **In the same way, what you fertilize your mind with will eventually lead to producing a lot or a little fruit, depending on what you pour into your *Inner Game.***

What's the goal of your *Inner Game*? What destiny should you aim for? How do you become your Best Self? Are you doing things that are meaningful to you and are a good fit for your interest and talents? Do you honor your commitments to yourself and to others?

It should be about much more than money, as any wealthy person will tell you. In fact, if you do a modern survey of the wealthy, you will find that many of them gained money almost accidentally. They made the first objective for their Outer Game to be a more complete, better and happier person. The wealth followed later.

In some cases, the wealth that followed was snatched away by forces outside of the person's control, but eventually those with superior *Inner Game* rebounded stronger than before. The very rich are indeed different; some have gained millions and lost millions too. It's what they do after their losses that determine their ultimate success, and that's where *Inner Game* comes in.

Bad things don't "just happen to you"… Bad things have impact when you aren't ready, aren't in control, aren't knowledgeable enough, or didn't take action. The point is to see yourself as being IN CONTROL.

Can you see the difference in attitude? It's not a whiny or complaining attitude. Things like complaining imply that we don't have the power to fix things and make our own reality. It's a question of "figuring out what to do."

Take a second to think of a skill that you're good at…

It could be a sport, it could be some type of game, it could be something relating to work or anything you can think of. For example, let's say you're good at golf. A good golfer will rarely blame his club, the wind, an injury or anything other than himself when he plays a bad shot. If he plays a bad shot he'll instantly try and figure out what he did wrong in terms of his swing or any other factor so that he can correct it for the next shot.

Part of great *Inner Game* is an attitude of "being in control. "And I imagine that whatever skills you're good at you have a similar attitude of constantly trying to figure out what you can do to do it better, because you realize that *YOU* are the one in control of the results with that skill. Well the same is true for any aspect of your life.

Another key part of great *Inner Game* is savoring the moments, the good, the bad, even the ugly. Squeezing out all of the pleasure in a moment. When given lemons, make lemonade. After all, much of life is a collection of moments. Use the fear of mediocrity to stay on the path of greatness.

To build and nurture your *Inner Game* feed your mind a daily dose of positive information or business improvement ideas in the areas of your passions. You can read 30 minutes in the morning and/or 30 minutes in evening to help take your *Inner Game* to a higher level. Remember, a person who does not read is no better off than a person who cannot read.

Take a look at Table 4 on the following page. This table summarizes well the choices you will need to make to create a winning *Inner Game* and attract prosperity to you like the multi-millionaires do. The correct choice of attitude in each category should be obvious, but that does not mean that adopting the strengthening attitude is easy. How badly do you want to be rich? That desire will move the needle in each of these categories as quickly as you want it to.

This table might appear to be overly simple, yet each attitude choice can run as deep as an ocean.

Table 4. Design Your Inner Game

Strengthening Attitudes	Weakening Attitudes
"I create my life."	"Life happens to me."
Play to win	Play not to lose
"I know what I want"	"I don't know what I really want"
Think BIG	Think small
Focus on opportunities	Focus on obstacles
Admire successful people	Resent successful people
Friends are successful	Friends are not successful
Grow self larger than my problems	Reduce self to be smaller than my problems
Paid based on results	Paid based on time
"I control money"	"Money controls me"
"Money works for me"	"I work for money"
"I persist through fear"	"Fear stops or delays my actions"
Continuous learning	"I already know everything"

How did you grade? When were you forced to admit that you are in the right-hand column? What do you plan to do to get into the left-hand column in all 14 choices?

This book builds on, condenses and updates the principles used in *Think and Grow Rich*, applying that wisdom from the early part of the 20th Century to the 21st Century. Among the timeless truths discussed in that book are:

- Know what you want; those who want to be successful will know precisely what they want and have an ardent desire to attain it. Hill encouraged his readers to hold an image of themselves in a place where they desired to be financially and personally, and promised them that they would be drawn towards that image.

- Practice continual visualization: think about your goals every morning and affirm that you will accomplish them, envisioning what your world will look like when you have reached your aims. Dwell on this photo or short movie often.

- Never stop learning: attend seminars and webinars, devour podcasts, read widely and play books on CD or your iPod when travelling, fire up that Kindle screen on the plane, talk to other successful people and mine their brains for knowledge.

- Make a plan with the help of trusted, successful associates: draw a map of how you will get from Point A to Point B. Get input from your closest advisors and take the time to brainstorm before setting a plan in motion. Put your desire into motion. Then track your progress in your DayTimer or mobile device.

- Persist through all roadblocks; if you are going to maintain your vision, you will need to have the attitude that *NOTHING* will cause you to give up. As you cling to your original vision, hold your plan loosely. It might need to be tweaked as you adapt to new circumstances. Again, call in advisors if you decide to initiate major changes

- Believe that your future is bright; this can also be called bedrock confidence, the idea that the future will be better than the present as you adopt the attitudes in the above table. This unflinching confidence has helped many people weather anything that life throws at them. It will be a key to your success, too.

Are the rich very different from you and me? Yes and no. They are human beings like you and me, and many do not have extraordinary talents or intellects.

However, you might not be like them at present because they consistently live in the left-hand column of the table above. Most have an iron-clad *Inner Game,* and this eventually causes all competitors and obstacles to crumble.

F. Scott Fitzgerald's contention that the rich are all rich from birth may have been true in his era, but it is very misleading in today's world. Today, more than ever around the world, people are developing their *Inner Game* and amassing fortunes. They play to win and think big. They steer their life course rather than letting circumstances dictate where they will end up. They know what they want and focus on opportunities to get there.

They spend time around successful people, get to know them, and they are paid on the basis of results, not their time. As they grow their bank accounts, they never let their money control them, and they persist in their vision even if large amounts are subtracted due to unforeseen circumstances.

Successful people never let fear stop them from doing something, and they never stop learning, either. These are the basic attitudes that contribute to an *Inner Game* that can change your destiny.

Resources

www.RobertRinger.com

www.RaisingWealthyKidsBook.com.

Endnotes

---

[1] http://www.baseball-almanac.com/hitting/hibavg4.shtml

[2] http://www.ssa.gov/policy/docs/statcomps/income_pop55/2010/incpop10.pdf

[3]

[iv] The most recent Dalbar findings can be analyzed here: http://www.moneynews.com/InvestingAnalysis/Dalbar-Harvey-individual-investors/2013/03/11/id/494045, retrieved 7/30/13.

[v] http://money.cnn.com/2012/03/02/pf/efficient_market.moneymag/index.htm, retrieved 7/30/13

[vi] http://www.cnbc.com/id/100858406, retrieved 7/30/13

[vii] http://www.theglobeandmail.com/report-on-business/rob-magazine/dont-believe-buffett-buy-and-hold-investing-is-dead/article10396622/, retrieved 7/30/13

[viii] www.DowTheoryLetters.com

[ix] There are many other types of alternative investments. These could include Real Estate Investment Trusts (REITS), hedge funds, managed futures, private equity, venture capital, limited partnerships, wine, art, and antiques. Most alternative investments are very illiquid, and require a special set of due diligence and expertise.

[x] "The original Dream Team, the U.S. basketball team that won the gold medal at the 1992 Olympics in Barcelona, was a phenomenon on and off the court. It mattered not that it dominated the Olympic competition, beating its eight opponents by an average of 44 points. What was important was that the Dream Team, the first U.S. Olympic team to include NBA stars, gave fans a glimpse of basketball at its finest, and an entire world responded." Source www.NBA.com.